Rull

HOW TO GE
HOTELS & C

In this Series

Other titles in preparation

How To...

GET A JOB IN HOTELS & CATERING

An international guide to employment opportunities

Mark Hempshell

How To Books

By the same author in this series

How to Get a Job in Europe
How to Get a Job in France
How to Get a Job in Travel & Tourism

British Library Cataloguing in Publication Data
A catalogue record for this book is available from the British Library.

© Copyright 1995 by Mark Hempshell.

First published in 1995 by How To Books Ltd, Plymbridge House, Estover Road, Plymouth PL6 7PZ, United Kingdom. Tel: Plymouth (01752) 735251/ 695745. Fax: (01752) 695699. Telex: 45635.

Note: The material contained in this book is set out in good faith for general guidance and no liability can be accepted for loss or expense incurred as a result of relying in particular circumstances on statements made in the book. The law and regulations are complex and liable to change, and readers should check the current position with the relevant authorities before making personal arrangements.

Typeset by Concept Communications (Design & Print) Ltd, Crayford, Kent. Printed and bound by The Cromwell Press Ltd, Broughton Gifford, Melksham, Wiltshire.

Preface

What do the five-star hotel in the centre of town, the guest house down the road, McDonalds in the High Street and the Egon Ronay-rated restaurant have in common? What is the link between your local pub, local hospital, a motorway service station and an oil rig?

The answer is simply that they are all, in some way, involved in the hotel and catering industry. They may all serve very different types of customers, in a very different way, but they are basically all in the same business.

This example serves to show what a vast industry hotels and catering is. It is one of the very few industries that is present in almost every city, town and village in the work. Not many other types of business, if any, can say that.

This is probably one of the reasons that hotel and catering work is becoming an increasingly popular career choice. People who enter this industry — and who are good at it — are unlikely to ever be short of an interesting or exciting opportunity. Whatever your reasons for wanting to work in hotels and catering — an exciting work atmosphere, good promotion prospects or opportunities to travel — people will always need something to eat and a place to stay.

It is because of the vast size of this industry that we have produced this book. If anything, there are too many choices, options and sources of information available. It's easy to get lost. The aim of this book is to act as a single, simple guide to all the opportunities on offer in the UK and worldwide.

The 1990s is a period of great change for hotel and catering businesses. New qualifications are being introduced, new working practices, such as multi-skilling, are now being developed, and new professional standards are being set. So this book aims to cover not only the opportunities that are on offer today, but those that will be on offer tomorrow.

This is an industry that is expanding fast, and internationally too. Nowadays there is a high level of cross-border co-operation, and a tendency for companies to have operations in several countries. So not only can you work on hotels and catering in your own town or city, but also in many countries around the world too!

I don't know exactly what you would like to do — maybe you would like to work in a top hotel in London or Paris, or maybe you would like to run your own fast food operation. But, whatever it is, you are unlikely to run short of choice and opportunities in this industry!

With thanks to all the organisations who have provided accurate information for this book including the Hotel, Catering and Institutional Management Association, the Hotel and Catering Training Company, Forte, Hilton, Pizza Hut, Welcome Break, Whitbread, Catering and Allied and City & Guilds.

The information in this book was as up to date as possible at the time of writing. However, details are subject to change and readers are cautioned to check the current position before making arrangements.

Mark Hempshell

Contents

List of Illustrations

IS THIS YOU?

Hotel manager   Hotel section manager
                  Hotel executive manager
Receptionist   Office clerk
                  Telephone operator
Reservations clerk   Cashier
                       Porter
Bellboy   Doorman
                       Valet
Concierge   Night porter
                   Housekeeper
Room attendant   Cleaning staff
                  Linen room manager
Linen room assistant   Linen room supervisor
                   Sales executive
Marketing executive   Conference organiser
                    Entertainer
Service/maintenance staff   Personnel officer
                  Training officer
Accountant   Catering unit manager
              Catering section manager
Catering executive manager   Restaurant manager
                     Head waiter
Waiter   Wine waiter
                     Bar waiter
Room service waiter   Bar staff
                     Head chef
Sous chef   Chef de partie
                    Commis chef
Trainee chef   Kitchen porter
                  Kitchen assistant
Cook   Catering assistant
              Counter food service assistant

1
Is Hotel and Catering the Job for You?

IS HOSPITALITY FOR YOU?

Another name for the hotel and catering industry is the hospitality industry. This explains quite well the sort of person you need to be if you are to be successful.

Hospitality is a **people** business, where very little is automated or mass produced. In almost every job in hotels and catering you'll be working closely with people, whether the public or your work colleagues. This applies whether you work in a hotel, restaurant, pub or fast food outlet.

If you're not hospitable, who'll want to be served by, or work with, you?

Of course, there is rather more to it than that. But this is one of the most important things you can know about working in hotels and catering. In so many cases in the hospitality industry it's the atmosphere of a place — the smile and the friendly welcome — that draws customers back.

THE ADVANTAGES AND DISADVANTAGES OF WORKING IN HOTELS AND CATERING

The pros

● An exciting work environment, especially in a top class establishment or abroad.

● The industry has a very good reputation for its thorough, professional training.

● The hospitality industry is an expanding industry. The skills you learn will always be in demand.

● If you are good you can move up the career ladder very quickly. (There are top chefs and hotel managers who are still in their 20s).

- Some jobs offer the opportunity to live and work in foreign countries.

- Rates of pay are comparable with, or better than, any other industry.

The cons
- Some jobs are 'behind the scenes' and, even in a top hotel or restaurant, the staff don't get the same luxury treatment as the customers!

- There is lots of competition for the vacancies. You will need to be determined if you want to get a job.

- Some jobs involve very long hours and modest pay, especially when you start out.

- In some jobs you must start at the bottom and work your way up. Promotion is given on merit only.

- Some jobs never offer you the chance to travel.

TYPES OF WORK YOU COULD BE DOING

The hospitality industry offers a very wide range of employment opportunities.

Types of business
There are two types of business to choose from:

- **Hotels:** Hotels provide somewhere to stay, whether for holidaymakers or business travellers. The hotel industry includes large international hotels, resort complexes, small local hotels, and even guest houses and inns.

- **Catering:** Anywhere which serves food or drink is a catering outlet. This includes restaurants within hotels, restaurants outside hotels, cafes, fast food outlets and takeaways, pubs, bars and motorway service areas. Also part of the catering industry are dining rooms and canteens in factories, offices, schools and hospitals.

Types of work

There are six types of work to choose from:

- **Food preparation:** Staff working in food preparation include chefs, cooks and kitchen porters.

- **Food and drink service:** Staff working in this area include waiters, restaurant managers, bar staff and counter staff.

- **Housekeeping:** Staff working in this area include room attendants, cleaners and housekeepers.

- **Reception:** Staff working in this area include receptionists, telephonists, reservations staff and porters.

- **Administrative, management and sales:** Staff working in this area include hotel managers, area managers, office clerks, personnel officers, accountants, training officers and sales representatives.

- **Support:** Staff working in this area include maintenance staff, security staff, drivers and storekeepers.

Types of employer

There are three types of employer to choose from:

- **Sole traders:** People who own their own hotel or restaurant and usually work in it as well, employing a small number of other people to help them.

- **Small groups:** Companies which own a small chain of hotels or catering units, often in just one part of the country.

- **Large groups:** Companies which owns hotels or catering units all over the country, and perhaps abroad too. These companies often own several well known brand names. Also included in this category are public authorities, such as schools and hospitals which run catering operations.

It is a good idea to think about what sort of work might suit you now. However, try to be flexible. Nowadays the concept of multi-skilling is becoming popular. This means people are trained to do several different jobs and so can move between different types of business operation easily.

If you are interested in working in tourist resorts, with airlines or on cruise ships, then we suggest you read *How to Get a Job in Travel and Tourism: An international guide to employment opportunities,* also available from How To Books.

JOB PROSPECTS

The hospitality industry is very well established. Inns began to open up to serve travellers as far back as the middle ages, and a few of them are still in business today!

The 1980s was a boom time for the industry. During this decade most people found they had more money to spend, and more leisure time to fill. Holidays at home and abroad, and eating out, were the ideal way to spend this extra time and cash.

Today 2.4 million people work in the hospitality industry in the UK. This is expected to grow by at least 170,000 people over the next five years alone. Despite the recession most of the large companies involved in the industry in the UK expect to expand over the next few years, and many of them have plans to expand internationally.

Unlike many industries, hospitality is not something that can be easily automated or mass produced. The personal, friendly touch will always be needed, and this calls for a regular intake of new, enthusiastic people.

WHAT YOU CAN EXPECT TO BE PAID

Rates of pay for beginners in hotel and catering work are often thought of as being low, involving hard work over long hours. This is not really true today and rates of pay in hospitality compare favourably with most other industries.

In many jobs in hospitality you are paid according to your ability and effort rather than your age or length of service. For example, there are top chefs and hotel managers still in their 20s and 30s and earning some of the highest salaries in the industry.

In the UK many staff get tips or bonuses on top of a reasonable basic wage. However, in some other countries this is not the case. Staff are paid only a very small basic wage and must rely on tips to make a reasonable income.

Fringe benefits offered to staff working in this industry include free uniforms, free meals whilst on duty and free or low cost live-in accommodation where appropriate. Some companies offer discounts on food and accommodation at other hotels and restaurants within their group.

Some examples of pay

- A new waiter earns a minimum of £3.17 per hour and also receives tips. In places where good tips are paid this can sometimes double the weekly wage.

- A junior chef earns between £12-£14,000 per year. The average wage for a senior chef is £28,000 per year.

- A hotel receptionist earns £3.50 per hour on average.

- A hotel housekeeper, in charge of a small team of chambermaids, earns between £10-£14,000 per year, depending on the size of the hotel.

- There is no standard rate of pay for a hotel manager. It all depends on how good you are and the size of the hotel. The average salary is £20-£24,000 per year. Some top hotel managers earn around £60,000 per year.

These rates of pay apply to the UK. Rates of pay in other countries may be much more, or much less, depending on the country.

HOW TO GET A JOB ABROAD

The hotel and catering industry is a global industry and so jobs are on offer in most countries. Even the eastern European countries now have a thriving industry, with privately owned hotels and restaurants opening all the time.

However, it is important to note that, while a lot of people in the industry here in the UK would like to work abroad, a majority of the jobs with British companies are based here in the UK. In order to keep costs down most UK companies who have businesses overseas recruit most of their staff locally and only send people to work abroad when it is absolutely necessary.

If you would like to work abroad then you will also need to apply to foreign companies based in the country in which you wish to work. This book covers jobs with both UK companies and foreign companies.

TRY THIS SELF-TEST . . . .

How to tell if hotels and catering is for you

Answer these questions

Do you like working with people? YES/NO

Do you have a service-orientated attitude?
(That is, you enjoy serving people and looking
after them.) YES/NO

Can you work well as a member of a team? YES/NO

But do you also like working on your own
initiative when necessary? YES/NO

Are you willing to work evenings, weekends or
even during the night? YES/NO

Are you willing to work your way up, and do all
the most basic jobs that need to be done — even
if you eventually want to be manager? YES/NO

Comment
If you can honestly answer YES to all six questions then you
will probably be very well suited to the hotel and catering
industry.

2
About Skills, Experience, Qualifications and Training

WHAT PERSONAL SKILLS DO EMPLOYERS LOOK FOR?

As we said in Chapter 1, most jobs in the hotel and catering industry are about people — helping people, serving people in one of many ways, and working with other people as a close-knit team. As a result most employers prefer people with good personal skills. You should:

- be friendly and outgoing

- be able to get on well with all types of people

- enjoy team work

- be a good communicator

- have a service-minded attitude, and enjoy attending to other people's needs

- not mind working unusual hours or under pressure.

These are skills which it is useful to try and develop. If you are currently working in another industry then consider how you can develop these skills in your current job. If you are a student then think how you can develop them in your work. A part-time or holiday job in a hotel or catering establishment will also help you develop these skills.

WHAT EXPERIENCE WILL YOU NEED?

No particular experience is needed to start a career in the hotel and catering industry. Most employers will take on completely inexperienced people for trainee positions assuming you have the qualifications required. There are very few hotel and catering employers who

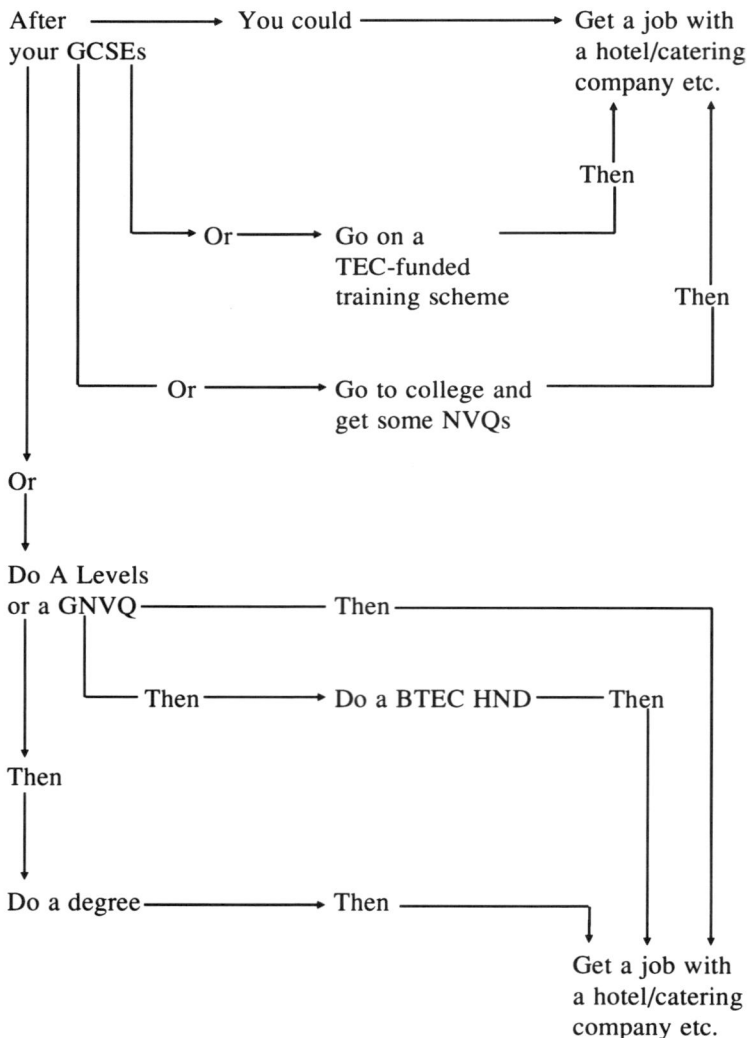

HOW TO GET INTO THE HOTEL AND CATERING INDUSTRY

A Guide for School Leavers

Start here

After your GCSEs → You could → Get a job with a hotel/catering company etc.

Or → Go on a TEC-funded training scheme → Then → Get a job with a hotel/catering company etc.

Or → Go to college and get some NVQs → Then

Or

Do A Levels or a GNVQ → Then

Then → Do a BTEC HND → Then

Then

Do a degree → Then

Get a job with a hotel/catering company etc.

do not have organised training schemes which train staff to their own particular standards, and so prior experience is not necessarily an advantage.

Many employers today train their staff by the 'work your way up' method. Most hotel managers have, at some time, worked in all the different departments of a hotel and some even started on the front desk or in the restaurant.

Experience gained in other industries is useful for some hotel and catering jobs. For example, those with experience in personnel, training, finance, accountancy, administration and sales and marketing can often transfer quite easily to the hospitality industry.

QUALIFICATIONS YOU NEED

Most employers in the hospitality industry require you to have a good general education as a minimum requirement. Anyone still at school and planning a career should make sure they get the best GCSE grades possible. Some jobs cannot be entered unless you have these.

The actual qualifications required vary from job to job and more specific information is given on qualifications in Chapter 3. Those at school and choosing their subject options are strongly advised to check with employers as to what subjects they will require.

How to use any qualifications
No qualifications: Job opportunities for those with no qualifications will always be more limited, although the industry does offer some potential for those without qualifications to start at the bottom and work their way up.

With GCSEs: Four GCSEs at grades A-C is sufficient to gain entry on the training schemes and take most junior positions offered by many employers in the industry. It is still possible to work your way up into a senior position by starting at this point — if you are good enough.

With A levels: Two or three A levels will get you into trainee schemes, including management trainee schemes, with many companies, but vocational qualifications (NVQs, GNVQs and BTEC) are often more useful for those wishing to work in hospitality.

With GNVQs: A GNVQ (General National Vocational Qualification) in Hospitality and Catering is available at Intermediate and Advanced level (from September 1994) and Foundation level (from 1995) at some schools and many colleges.

Intermediate Hospitality and Catering

Mandatory units
Unit 1   Investigating hospitality and catering
Unit 2   Customer service in hospitality and catering
Unit 3   Providing front office and accommodation operations
Unit 4   Providing food and drink

Optional units
Unit 5   Costing and pricing
Unit 6   Investigate hygiene in hospitality and catering
Unit 7   Contribute to a service or function
Unit 8   Purchasing and storage of commodities and materials

Advanced Hospitality and Catering

Mandatory units
Unit 1   Investigating the hospitality and catering industry
Unit 2   Human behaviour and resources
Unit 3   Providing customer care in hospitality and catering
Unit 4   Food and drink service systems
Unit 5   Food preparation and cooking
Unit 6   Purchasing, costing and finance
Unit 7   Accommodation operations
Unit 8   Reception and front office operations in hospitality

Optional units
Unit 9   Human resource management
Unit 10   Financial resources
Unit 11   Supervising operations for a service or function
Unit 12   Investigating supervision
Unit 13   Promoting products and service
Unit 14   The hospitality and catering environment
Unit 15   Science in the hospitality and catering industry
Unit 16   Obtain information about non-routine and daily
           activities by listening (Languages Lead Body
           standards)
Unit 17   Deal orally with varied daily activities (Languages
           Lead Body standards)

Fig. 1. GNVQ Hospitality & Catering Course Units.

With NVQs: Vocational qualifications are very important in the hospitality industry and it is essential to have a vocational qualification to get some jobs. In the past City & Guilds qualifications were asked for by most employers. Now, NVQs (National Vocational Qualifications) are being introduced and courses which grant these are offered by many colleges.

With a degree or HND: Those entering hotel and catering with a degree or BTEC HND usually get into management posts and many companies in the industry operate a graduate entry scheme.

In Scotland: The Scottish equivalents of these qualifications (SCEs, SVQs, GSVQs and SCOTVEC) apply.

MORE ABOUT BTECS AND GNVQS

The system of vocational courses and qualifications available to those wishing to work in the hotel and catering industry is currently changing. In the past, those wishing to work in the industry were recommended to take a BTEC First Certificate or Diploma, BTEC National Certificate or Diploma, or a BTEC Higher National Certificate. These are still valid and will be accepted by employers for the foreseeable future. However, students now starting at college (from autumn 1994) will instead be offered a GNVQ in Hospitality and Catering and this will become the new standard industry qualification.

The BTEC HND (Higher National Diploma) qualification in Hotel, Catering and Institutional Management is still available and has not been replaced by GNVQs.

In Scotland the situation is rather different. Here students can choose between a SCOTVEC National Certificate, Higher National Certificate or Higher National Diploma AND a GSVQ in Hospitality.

The units you will study in GNVQ Hospitality and Catering are listed on page 20. The Advanced Level GNVQ is broadly equivalent to two A levels. The Intermediate Level GNVQ is equivalent to four GCSEs at grades A-C.

Other vocational qualifications may be acceptable for some hotel and catering jobs, for example, the GNVQ in Business.

Addresses of colleges which offer BTEC and GNVQ and equivalent Scottish courses are listed in Chapter 5.

MORE ABOUT DEGREES

Degree Level Courses: Several universities and colleges offer degree level courses in Hotel and Catering. However, a number of other degrees are acceptable for some jobs in hospitality — for example, Leisure, Tourism, Business or Food Science, depending on the actual job you wish to do — and the HCIMA (Hotel, Catering and Institutional Management Association) have an exceptional entry scheme allowing graduates of other disciplines to obtain a recognised hotel and catering qualification.

Many hotel and catering courses include a year spent working in industry. In some cases this is spent working abroad.

A number of universities also offer postgraduate and other specialised courses so that those with a degree or experience in the industry can obtain further qualifications.

A list of universities and colleges offering degree level courses is given on page 99.

Those still at school and interested in taking a college or university course should take advice from their school or careers service as to the most appropriate course for their abilities and future plans.

MORE ABOUT NATIONAL VOCATIONAL QUALIFICATIONS

Vocational qualifications are regarded as being very important in the hospitality industry; in some cases it can be difficult to obtain certain jobs unless you hold certain specific vocational qualifications.

At the moment, as in many other industries, there is a transitional period in which the older industry qualifications, such as City & Guilds, are being superseded by the new National Vocational Qualifications or NVQs (SVQs in Scotland).

However, those who have or are studying for the older qualifications will find they are still valid for the foreseeable future. In job advertisements you will often see requirements for City & Guilds qualifications stated. NVQs will begin to be requested in due course.

Obtaining your NVQs

NVQs can be obtained in two ways:

1. By studying for them at college. Many colleges now offer NVQ courses for those wishing to make a career in hotels and catering. Colleges offering these courses are listed on page 101.

2. By obtaining them once you are working in a hotel or catering establishment.

Training

Most employers in hotel and catering place a great deal of emphasis on training. As part of this, most large employers will allow you to obtain NVQs, and other specialist industry qualifications, at work. This training is given either in the workplace or on college courses. Where employers do not offer industry qualifications, employees can obtain them through a distance learning programme provided by the HCIMA (the Hotel, Catering and Institutional Management Association) and other professional associations.

Skills units
Wherever you obtain your NVQs, training, study and assessment for them is divided into units each covering particular skills. Each unit can be collected at your own pace until you have gained enough to be granted the NVQ. Although NVQs involve some written tests, most tests comprise a project or assessment of your work in your workplace. You will be assessed either by your own employer or a local college. NVQs in Catering and Hospitality are issued by BTEC (and SCOTVEC) and the City & Guilds organisation in association with the HCIMA and the Hotel and Catering Training Company (HCTC).

Four levels of NVQ
NVQs in Catering and Hospitality are currently offered at four levels and employees can start at whatever level is most appropriate to their needs and job status; it is not always necessary to start at Level 1 and work up. The chart on page 24 illustrates how the NVQs relate to each other.

TRAINING AND QUALIFICATIONS AVAILABLE FROM THE PROFESSIONAL BODIES

HCIMA qualifications
Some, but not all, supervisory and management jobs in hospitality require applicants, especially non-graduates, to hold a HCIMA (Hotel, Catering and Institutional Management Association) qualification.

The HCIMA Professional Certificate is for those who work in, or who hope to get, supervisory posts. The HCIMA Professional Diploma is for those with supervisory or junior management experience who want to aim for more senior management posts. Both are studied for once you are working in the industry.

Prior entry requirements for HCIMA courses vary and include both

JUNIOR/MIDDLE MANAGEMENT LEVEL — 4 / 4

Catering and hospitality management
- (Reception)
- (Food and drink service) — **On licensed premises management**
- (Housekeeping)
- (Food prep and cooking)
- MANAGEMENT SKILLS

SUPERVISORY/SKILLED LEVEL — 3 / 3

Catering and hospitality supervisory management
- (Reception)
- (Food and drink service) — **On licensed premises supervisory management**
- (Housekeeping)
- (Food prep and cooking)
- ADVANCED CRAFT/SUPERVISORY SKILLS

SUPERVISORY/SKILLED LEVEL — 3

Catering and hospitality
- (Food preparation and cooking; Kitchen and Larder Work)
- (Food preparation and cooking; Patisserie and Confectionery)

Fig. 2. NVQs in Catering & Hospitality: map of qualifications.

SEMI-SKILLED LEVEL	2	**Catering and hospitality** (Reception)	(Serving food and drink – restaurant) (Serving food and drink – bar) (General)	(Housekeeping)	(Food prep and cooking)	CRAFT SKILLS
OPER-ATIVE LEVEL	1	**Catering and hospitality** (Reception and portering)	(Serving food and drink– bar) (Serving food and drink – table/tray) (Serving food and drink – counter) (Serving food and drink – take away) (Guest services)	(Housekeeping)	(Food prep and cooking – general) (Food prep and cooking – quick service)	BASIC SKILLS

academic qualifications and prior experience in the industry. Various programmes of study are available including full-time at college, sandwich courses, part-time at college (one day per week) and distance learning (home study) courses.

HCIMA also has an exceptional entry scheme which allows graduates of a discipline other than hotels and catering, or HND holders, to gain a HCIMA Diploma.

For further details of HCIMA membership, qualifications, courses, and a list of colleges which offer them, contact: HCIMA, 191 Trinity Road, London SW17 7HN. Tel: (0181) 672 4251.

Other associations

In addition to HCIMA a number of other professional associations offer training courses leading to professional memberships and diplomas. For example, the Wine and Spirit Education Trust offers a Certificate, Higher Certificate and Diploma in wine keeping, retailing and service. Although most of these qualifications are not mandatory they can help when applying for jobs or aiming to secure promotion.

Details of courses and qualifications can be obtained from the associations which are listed in Chapter 5. However, since they are all intended for people with work experience in hospitality it is not necessary for students or newcomers to the industry to have them.

TRAINING OPPORTUNITIES FOR YOUNG PEOPLE

Youth Training schemes are available for those aged 16 or 17 who want to make a career in the hospitality industry.

A special scheme is run by the Hotel and Catering Training Company (HCTC). HCTC can organise training, study at college, and work experience with employers in the industry. Local Training and Enterprise Councils (TECs, or LECs in Scotland) and enterprise companies in some areas also have schemes in association with local partners, or fund trainees on the HCTC scheme. Each scheme lasts for up to two years.

In some cases those who join the scheme are trainees and are paid a training allowance. There is no guarantee of a job at the end. In other cases those who join the scheme are employed by an employer, receive a full wage, and then have a guaranteed job at the end of the scheme. In both cases there is an opportunity to obtain the NVQs in Catering and Hospitality.

Those interested in these schemes should make enquiries with their school careers service, local TEC or the HCTC: Hotel and Catering Training Company, International House, High Street, Ealing, London W5 5DB. Tel: (0181) 579 2400.

COMMERCIAL TRAINING ORGANISATIONS

A number of commercial training organisations offer courses in various aspects of hotel and catering. For example, the Hotel Career Centre offers a Hotel and Catering Diploma, Travel and Tourism Diploma, Hotel and Catering Management Diploma, Hotel Operations Certificate, Travel and Tourism Certificate and a Cookery Certificate.

These courses are advertised from time to time in the national newspapers. A fee is payable. Some of these courses provide you with a formal qualification, such as a BTEC or NVQ, but others do not and so you should check whether the end qualification is likely to be accepted by employers before taking it.

WHAT IF I WANT TO WORK ABROAD?

UK qualifications are not always accepted by employers in foreign countries and this should be considered when applying for a job with a foreign employer.

The main exception to this is that UK degrees are considered equivalent to locally issued degrees in all the countries of the European Union (previously known as the European Community). Some City & Guilds, BTEC, GNVQs and NVQs which relate to work in hospitality are regarded as similar to other European qualifications according to the CEDEFOP organisation which harmonises qualifications within the EU. Currently, GCSEs and A levels are not.

Further details of this are given in Chapter 6, or can be obtained from: Employment Department, Qualifications and Standards Branch, Room E454, Moorfoot, Sheffield S1 4PQ. Tel: (0114) 2594144.

Do you need to speak a foreign language?

Whether or not you need a foreign language to work in hotel and catering depends on exactly what job you hope to do and where you want to work.

Most UK based staff do not need to be able to speak a foreign language. Those who hope to work in a major international hotel or restaurant will find knowledge of a foreign language useful, especially French, German, Italian and Japanese.

PERSONAL ASSESSMENT CHART

What skills do I have?

_____

_____

What skills do I need to get?

_____

_____

What qualifications do I have?

_____

_____

What qualifications do I need to get?

_____

_____

Do I need experience?
If so, how do I get it?

_____

_____

Do I need training?
If so, what training is most appropriate for me?

_____

_____

Do I need a foreign language?
If so, how do I learn it?

_____

_____

Do I need a visa and work permit?

_____

_____

The next chapter will explain the skills, experience and qualifications needed for the job or jobs which you find interesting.

Staff who work in locations abroad, such as receptionists or managers, may need to speak a foreign language, but it very much depends on the country in question and the job. In the popular tourist countries of Spain and Greece, for example, such is the volume of UK tourists that it is possible to get jobs with no local foreign language knowledge, especially if they are casual or seasonal jobs. However, knowledge of a foreign language will always be an advantage.

In most cases employers look for how well you actually know the language rather than academic qualifications in it, although an A level in a foreign language is sometimes requested.

What permits are needed to work abroad?

If you wish to work abroad then work visas, work permits and residence permits are usually needed. In most cases your employer will help with these, but some information on how to obtain them in the various countries is given later.

The European Union

UK passport holders do not need a work permit or visa to work in any country which is part of the European Union (EU). These are Belgium, Denmark, France, Germany, Greece, Ireland, Italy, Luxembourg, Netherlands, Portugal and Spain, as well as the UK.

This arrangement is being extended to countries which are members of the European Economic Area (Austria, Finland, Iceland, Norway, Sweden, Switzerland). However, at the moment a work visa and permit may still be needed. Details should be obtained from the appropriate Embassy before going abroad.

Even if working in one of the EU countries you will need a residence permit. This should be applied for within three months of arriving abroad. Details of where are given later. As long as you have a job it will be granted as a matter of right.

THE HOUSE WINE, SIR?

3
A Job for You in
Hotels and Catering

THE JOBS YOU CAN DO

Whatever your skills, there is likely to be a job you can do in hotels and catering. This chapter outlines the duties, qualifications needed (if any), pay and conditions of the following jobs:

In hotels
- Manager
- Section manager
- Executive manager
- Receptionist
- Office staff
- Telephone operator
- Reservations clerk
- Cashier
- Porter/Uniformed staff
- Housekeeper
- Room attendant
- Cleaning staff
- Linen room staff
- Sales and marketing staff
- Conference/banqueting/exhibition staff
- Entertainment staff
- Service and maintenance staff
- Personnel and training staff
- Accountant

In catering
- Unit manager
- Section manager
- Executive manager
- Restaurant manager
- Waiter

- Bar staff
- Chef
- Kitchen porter/kitchen assistant
- Cook
- Catering assistant
- Counter food service assistant
- Cashier

JOBS IN HOTELS

Hotel Manager

What you do
The job of hotel manager — sometimes known as general manager — is one of the most prestigious in the hospitality industry. The hotel manager is in overall charge of running the hotel but, other than this, the work is very varied. The manager of a 600 room international class hotel is basically an executive, supervising a team of department managers. On the other hand the manager of a small 20 room hotel might be expected to work on the reception desk or in the kitchens as well.

Today, two of the main concerns of every hotel manager are customer care and ensuring that the hotel trades profitably.

What you need
To get a job as a hotel manager in a good quality hotel you will need either a BTEC HND or a degree in Hotel and Catering Management. This will get you onto the management training schemes operated by the main hotel groups. Some of these groups will accept A levels, GNVQs or other BTEC qualifications as well.

Most hotel managers start as trainee managers, section (or department) managers or assistant managers and are promoted to hotel manager on merit. Before you can apply for hotel manager posts you will usually need 2-5 years' experience as a minimum and, in some cases for non-graduates, the HCIMA Professional Diploma, which can also be studied for once you have found your first job.

Hotel managers must have a confident personality and be good at dealing with people, both staff and guests. Knowledge of a foreign language is an asset, but not essential.

How to find a job
Most of the main hotel groups, such as Forte and Hilton, and some larger, privately owned hotels, have organised management training

schemes. These are advertised in the Caterer and Hotelkeeper *Careers Guide* magazine and the *Handbook of Tourism*. However, if you are interested in becoming a hotel manager you should write to the hotel groups giving details of the qualifications you have (or are taking) and your experience (if any).

Some small hotels only employ hotel managers who are already trained or have experience. Jobs for experienced hotel managers are advertised in the national newspapers and *Caterer and Hotelkeeper* magazine.

Pay and conditions
Starting pay for a graduate trainee is in the region of £10-£12,000 per year. The average pay for an experienced manager is £20-£24,000 per year. There is no upper limit: it all depends on how good you are. Some top hotel managers earn £60,000 per year or more.

Where to find out more
Contact the hotel groups and ask for details of their management training schemes. HCIMA will provide details of HCIMA qualifications and membership. The British Tourist Authority have a useful careers booklet called *Graduates in Tourism and Leisure* and the English Tourist Board have a booklet called *Graduate Opportunities in Tourism and Leisure*.

Case history

Mark Matthews, age 23, Leeds: Management Trainee
'I first became interested in hotel management work when I was 15 or 16 and, although keen to go out and get a job there and then and work my way up, my careers teacher persuaded me to take my time. It turned out to be good advice because more and more companies nowadays are looking for graduates.

'I took my A levels (English, History and Economics) and then took a BA in Hospitality Business Management at what is now Leeds Metropolitan University. I didn't take the year-in-industry sandwich option but, looking back, I think this is something everyone should do if they can.

'With my degree I applied to several of the major hotel chains and had offers from three of them. I chose this company because, although they have an organised graduate entry scheme, there are virtually no limits. At the outset, and then at regular intervals, you sit down with the Training Manager and decide, together, where you would like to go, and where the company can best use your particular talents. Like most trainee managers I've done a stint in the kitchens, the restaurant, the bar and the housekeeping department!

'At the moment I'm a deputy duty manager here, which means I report to the general manager on a range of areas of responsibility, and also take charge of the hotel on a rota basis — often this is during the nights, but it can also be a busy Saturday afternoon. Even as a trainee you're not given just the easy jobs!

'The future? Another couple of years here to gain more experience. Then I'll be looking for my own hotel. Here, as with a lot of companies in the industry, there's no minimum age for management. If you can do the job well you'll get the promotion.'

Hotel section manager

What you do
Most large hotels employ section managers, although most small hotels do not. A section manager (or department manager) is in charge of a particular department within the hotel. Jobs which fall into this category include the room service manager, front office manager and, in large hotels, the restaurant manager, bar manager or conference and banqueting manager.

The job of section manager is a career position in its own right. Although some section managers eventually intend to become hotel managers many others intend to specialise in section management from the outset.

What you need
To get a job as a section manager you will usually need, at least, good A levels or a GNVQ, or a BTEC National Diploma (for those already holding this qualification). This will get you onto the training schemes operated by the main hotel groups. Some of these groups will expect a BTEC HND or degree.

These qualifications do not necessarily have to be in Hotel and Catering as long as you have particular aptitude for hospitality work, or previous relevant experience. Sometimes those without these qualifications but with extensive experience in hospitality (such as waiters or receptionists) can get accepted on section management training schemes.

Many section managers today also obtain the HCIMA Professional Diploma, which can be studied for once you have found your first job.

How to find a job
Most of the large and medium sized hotel groups have section man-

agement training schemes. These are advertised in the Caterer and Hotelkeeper *Careers Guide* magazine and the *Handbook of Tourism*. However, if you are interested in becoming a section manager you should write to the hotel groups giving details of the qualifications you have (or are taking) and your experience (if any).

Jobs for experienced section managers are advertised in the national newspapers and *Caterer and Hotelkeeper* magazine.

Pay and conditions
The average pay for a section manager in a medium sized hotel is £15-£18,000 per year. Bar and restaurant managers may earn more.

Where to find out more
Contact the hotel groups and ask for details of their management training schemes. HCIMA will provide details of HCIMA qualifications and membership. The British Tourist Authority have a useful careers booklet called *Graduates in Tourism and Leisure* and the English Tourist Board have a booklet called *Graduate Opportunities in Tourism and Leisure*.

Executive manager

What you do
The job of the executive manager is what is known as functional management. That is, the job is to manage the hotel group as a company rather than, as the hotel manager does, run an individual hotel. Some executive managers work in hotels but the majority work at head office.

Areas which an executive manager may take responsibility for include sales and marketing, finance, human resources (personnel) and property development. Some executive managers are area managers, in charge of the company's hotels in a particular region.

The executive manager is very much a businessman or woman rather than a hotel professional.

What you need
Executive managers must usually have a degree or a HND qualification as a minimum. This can be in Hospitality and Catering or some other business-orientated discipline.

If you lack these qualifications you can still enter this area of work if you have very extensive experience (usually a minimum of five years) in hospitality or a relevant area (such as personnel or finance) of some other industry.

Many would-be executive managers study for further professional qualifications. These include the HCIMA Diploma, the Institute of Management qualifications, or an MA, MSc or MBA.

How to find a job
Some executive managers gain their experience in another industry, or are promoted from hotel managers. The largest hotel and catering companies have training programmes for graduates aiming for executive positions. These jobs are rarely advertised and it is best to write to suitable companies for further details.

Pay and conditions
There is no standard rate of pay for executive managers, who can earn between £20,000 and £60,000 per year, or more, depending on their experience and ability. Such jobs are also likely to include substantial benefits such as company car and, with some companies, the opportunity to work abroad.

Where to find out more
Contact the hotel groups and ask for details of their management training schemes. *Careers and Training in Hotels, Catering and Tourism* by Roy Hayter of the Hotel and Catering Training Company (published by Butterworth Heinemann) has useful chapters on further qualifications and postgraduate study.

Hotel Receptionist

What you do
The hotel receptionist is the member of staff whom every guest meets first. As such, this job carries a great deal of importance and some prestige, and most hotels select and train their receptionists very carefully.

The work varies according to the size of the hotel. In a large hotel, where there will be a head receptionist and deputy receptionist as well, the work will mainly involve greeting guests and organising their check-in and check-out. In smaller hotels the receptionist will also answer the 'phone, accept reservations, answer queries and handle some of the office work.

What you need
Receptionists may be male or female. You must have a helpful and outgoing personality, together with a pleasant appearance. If you have

STRUCTURE

A two year programme planned to enable experience of all hotel concepts and head office functions.

The first ten months of the programme is designed to give all round general experience within CCH. The Corporate Trainee Manager will be trained to Gold Standard and be assessed to achieve recognition wherever possible.

SCHEDULE

5 Months — Country Club Hotels 'A'

— Reception/Reservations   — Bar and Cellar
— Restaurants   — Housekeeping
— Banqueting

(Approx. 4 weeks in each area)

5 Months — Country Club Hotels 'B'

Departments to be covered:
— Conference: Operations/Administration
— Golf and Leisure   — Poolside
— Kitchen   — Finance

(Approx. 4 weeks in each area)

5 Months — Lansbury Hotels

Head of Department role at a Lansbury Hotel. The location and role will depend on opportunities available at the time.

3 Months — Head Office

To include:

— Sales and Marketing   — Property
— Finance   — Operations
— Human Resources

Fig. 3. Example of a hotel management training programme.
(Thanks to the Whitbread Group of Hotels for supplying this example.)

<u>1 Month — Travel Inn</u>

To include time at Head Office and at both Standalone and Franchise operations.

<u>5 Months — Country Club Hotels</u>

Head of Department role at a Country Club Hotel. The location and role will depend on opportunities available at the time.

OFF JOB DEVELOPMENT

Through the two years the Corporate Trainee Managers will attend various courses to gain appropriate qualifications.
These should include:

— Craft Trainer Award
— Group Training Technique
— Basic Food Hygiene
— First Aid

— Sales Training
— Focused Interview Training
— Business Planning
   (Functional Manager level)
— Lotus 123

In addition to this, the Corporate Trainee Manager will be supported through 'The Capable Manager', an Open Business School programme leading to the Professional Certificate in Management. This will commence after 6 months. Enrolment on this programme will depend on successful performance to date.

PROSPECTS

At the end of the two years the Corporate Trainee Manager will take up a full time appointment as a line Manager within either a CCH or Lansbury Hotel. This will be dependent on opportunities available and successful performance throughout the programme.

Fig. 3. Continued.

prior experience of working with the public (for example in a shop) this will be an advantage.

Those wishing to work in a top hotel will find knowledge of a foreign language an asset, though not essential.

Most hotels expect their receptionists to have a good general education comprising, at least, four or five GCSEs (any subject). An NVQ Level 2 or 3 in Reception is useful, but not essential. This is similar to the City & Guilds 720 qualification which it replaces, and which some employers may still ask for.

How to find a job
Most hotels employ both trainee receptionists and experienced receptionists. Some opportunities are advertised in the *Careers Guide* magazine; also see your local newspapers. If you are interested in becoming a hotel receptionist you should also consider writing to the hotel groups and also small privately owned hotels.

School leavers interested in this type of work should look at the training programmes offered by the Hotel and Catering Training Company (HCTC) or your local TEC.

Pay and conditions
Pay for a receptionist varies between £7,000 and £12,000 depending on your experience and size of the hotel. Receptionists must be prepared to work shifts, including shifts at night and at the weekend.

Where to find out more
Write to the major hotel groups. The *Handbook of Tourism* and the *Careers Guide* magazine also provide further information about reception work.

Case history

Jane, age 20, Edinburgh: Hotel Receptionist
'I have always wanted to work in a hotel, so in my last year at school I kept a sharp eye out in the local papers for any vacancies, and wrote and applied for some of them **before** I had got my GCSE results. Three or four local hotels called me in for an interview and said that — yes — as long as I got good grades they would consider taking me on as a trainee receptionist. When the results came out I was very pleased to be offered a job at a privately-owned country house hotel about twenty minutes from where I live.

'My first few months in the job were a bit routine. I did a lot of filing and photocopying and general office work. Sometimes I wish I had gone on to college, but at least this way I received my training and got paid too!

'Gradually I was introduced to the various areas of the work, including telephone reception, reservations and guest accounts. Front desk work is the last area you cover — the head receptionist has to be sure you are competent — and confident — before they'll let you loose on the guests!

'After eight months I became a fully-fledged receptionist. A few months later I moved to a much larger hotel here in Edinburgh, where I still work. Although the wage is about the same, this company does give you the chance to obtain NVQs and other qualifications which, hopefully, will help me reach my goal of becoming head receptionist or reservations supervisor in the not-too-distant future.'

Hotel office staff

What you do
Only the medium sized and larger hotels have a substantial number of office staff. In the smallest hotels this work is done by the receptionists.

The job of the office staff is very varied. It includes typing, filing, computer work, telephone answering and basic accounts work. The job is very much like similar jobs in an office and does not involve dealing with guests.

What you need
Hotel office staff should have a good general education comprising four or five GCSEs, or experience in an office environment including a knowledge of typing, word processing, basic accounts and telephone work. A BTEC First or National qualification (for those already holding these), GNVQ in Hospitality and Catering, NVQ in Reception (or the older City and Guilds 720) is an advantage but not essential. Those holding the better qualifications may be able to gain promotion to front office manager in the future.

How to find a job
The best way to find a job is to check the advertisements in the local and national newspapers. School leavers interested in this type of work should look at the training programmes offered by the Hotel and Catering Training Company (HCTC) or your local TEC.

Pay and conditions
Rates of pay are similar to those for receptionists. Office staff mostly

work on a 9am-5pm, Monday to Friday basis, but may occasionally have to work at night or during the weekend.

Where to find out more
Write to the hotel groups. Useful information is also given in the *Careers Guide* magazine.

Hotel telephone operator

What you do
The telephone operator works only in the larger hotels. In smaller hotels this work will be done by the receptionist or office staff.

In a large, busy hotel the work of the telephone operator can be hectic. Although modern switchboards are largely automatic there are still incoming calls to be answered and directed, and calls to be placed for staff and guests, many of which may be overseas.

Good telephone operators are sometimes promoted to the job of front office manager.

What you need
Most hotel employers expect four or five good GCSEs (any subjects). Alternatively, those with experience as telephone operators in another type of industry are also employed. To work in a top hotel a knowledge of, and an A level in, another language (French, German, Italian or Japanese) is an advantage. You must have a helpful personality and a clear telephone voice.

How to find a job
Check the advertisements in the local and national newspapers. You should also consider writing to hotel groups and privately owned hotels. Some hotel groups have a telephone operations training course and will employ the inexperienced, but others do not.

Pay and conditions
Average pay is in the region of £3.50 per hour; higher in the case of those speaking a foreign language. Telephone operators must usually work shifts, including evenings and weekends, for which an extra payment is made.

Where to find out more
Write to the hotel groups. Useful information is also given in the *Careers Guide* magazine.

Hotel reservations clerk

What you do
The reservations clerk takes room reservations, usually over the 'phone. The clerk may work at individual hotels, or at a centralised booking centre, where they deal with calls from members of the public and travel agents. The work involves use of up-to-the-minute telecommunications and computer reservations equipment.

Reservations clerks do not merely advise on room availability. Most hotel groups have a very complicated room rate system with different rates applying to different rooms, different dates and different guests. The reservations clerk must interpret the guest's requirements and advise on the appropriate rate.

What you need
Most hotel employers expect four or five good GCSEs (any subjects). You should have a good telephone voice, be able to work accurately under pressure, and be able to use a keyboard. It is an advantage if you have a genuine interest in selling.

Good reservations clerks are sometimes promoted to the job of front office manager.

How to find a job
Check the advertisements in the *Careers Guide* magazine. You should also write to the hotel groups and also privately owned hotels. Some hotel groups have a training programme for those who wish to become reservations clerks and will employ people without any prior experience.

Pay and conditions
Rates of pay are similar to receptionists, office staff and telephonists. Reservations agents must also be prepared to work out of hours as many booking centres are open until late, seven days a week, and some operate 24 hours.

Where to find out more
Write to the hotel groups. Useful information is also given in the *Careers Guide* magazine and the *Handbook of Tourism. How to Get a Job in Travel and Tourism*, in this series, also describes other opportunities that are available in this type of work.

Hotel cashier

What you do
The hotel cashier's job is usually a very busy one. The cashier col-

lects and records payments from guests. They may also be involved with charging services to each guest's room account, providing a banking service to the hotel bars and restaurants, and making payments to suppliers and wages to staff. In the larger hotels they may also provide a *bureau de change* currency exchange service to guests.

What you need
Hotel cashiers should have a good general education comprising four or five GCSEs, including maths. A BTEC First or National qualification (for those already holding them), A levels, a GNVQ in Hospitality and Catering, NVQ in Reception (or the older City and Guilds 720) is an advantage but not essential. You must have a good head for figures and be able to work quickly and accurately.

Some hotels will employ those with experience in a bank, building society or experience of legal cashier work.

How to find a job
See local and national advertisements. You should also consider writing to the hotel groups and privately owned hotels. Some of them offer a training programme for those without experience who want to become cashiers.

Pay and conditions
A hotel cashier earns £8-£12,000 per year depending on the work involved and the level of responsibility. Usually cashiers work normal office hours only, although some out-of-hours work may be required.

Where to find out more
Write to the hotel groups.

Hotel porter/Uniformed staff

What you do
The hotel porters and door staff — also known as the uniformed staff — are often not regarded with the importance they deserve. However, they are an essential part of the team in any hotel. Apart from being some of the first members of staff the guests see, and so important ambassadors for their hotel, they do a range of jobs which make the hotel run smoothly.

Work carried out by the porters and door staff include welcoming guests, distributing luggage, security work, giving directions and providing an information and enquiry service.

Various jobs come within this category:

- **Porter**: The main work of the porters is to unload vehicles, assist guests with the check-in/check-out and distribute luggage. They also carry out other work such as delivering goods around the hotel, or setting up function rooms.

- **Bellboy**: A bellboy is basically a junior porter who distributes luggage and delivers messages, and is mostly only found in large international hotels.

- **Doorman**: Doormen are mostly found only in the larger international hotels. Their work includes keeping the door, welcoming guests, security control, as well as helping guests with parking or taxis.

- **Valet**: The job of the valet is to porter linen and laundry supplies. However, in some American and international hotels the valet is a car parking attendant.

- **Concierge**: The concierge desk is the hotel's information centre. A good concierge can answer a guest's questions on almost any aspect of the hotel's services, or facilities available in the local area. They can also book excursions, theatres, taxis, onward travel, and supply newspapers. In some hotels the concierge also keeps the room keys.

- **Night Porter**: The work of the night porter is very varied and not simply portering. At night they take over all the responsibilities of the door staff, including portering, door keeping and the concierge. In quieter hotels they may also operate the reception, answer the telephone, check-in late arrivals, do basic office work and provide room service.

In larger hotels all these jobs are carried out by different people. In a smaller hotel they are often combined.

What you need
Formal qualifications are not usually needed for any of these jobs, so long as you have the right personality. It would be an advantage to have the appropriate NVQs, but this is not essential. A Level 1 NVQ in Catering and Hospitality (Reception and Portering) is the appropriate NVQ for the job of Porter. A Level 2 or 3 NVQ in Catering and

Hospitality (Reception) is appropriate for the job of head porter, concierge or night porter.

All porters and door staff must have a good appearance and be physically fit. They should have a pleasant, helpful personality. Knowledge of a foreign language is always useful.

How to find a job
Some of the large hotel groups have an organised training programme for those wishing to work as porters and door staff. Write to them direct. Otherwise, check local and national newspapers. Many Job Centres and hotel employment agencies also handle this type of work, but mainly for those with some experience. Many small hotels do not employ those without experience.

Pay and conditions
Minimum pay is usually £3.50 per hour, or £7-£12,000 per year depending on the responsibility of the particular job. In some hotels, especially abroad, door staff may only receive a small basic wage, but are also given tips by guests. Shift work is also usually necessary, although only the night porters work during the night.

Where to find out more
Write direct to the hotel groups. The *Careers Guide* and *Handbook of Tourism* provide further information. The Society of Golden Keys is a professional organisation for the top head porters worldwide.

Hotel housekeeper

What you do
The housekeeping staff look after the accommodation in a hotel. It is important to remember that this is the whole reason for being of every hotel and the standards of work involved are usually very high. The housekeeping staff clean, service and restock the guest rooms and public areas and also deal with the large amount of linen that is used every day.

A small hotel will have a housekeeper who is in charge of the whole operation. In a larger hotel there will be a head housekeeper (and perhaps also a deputy head housekeeper) who is basically a manager and in charge of staff rotas, personnel, purchasing, budgeting and control of linen, and liaising with the reception and maintenance staff. There will also be several floor housekeepers who supervise the room attendants on each floor and ensure that the necessary standards are maintained.

What you need
Housekeepers should have an eye for detail, be able to maintain high standards and be good organisers. Few hotel companies set minimum qualifications but a GNVQ in Hospitality and Catering or appropriate NVQs would be an advantage. The NVQ in Catering and Hospitality (Housekeeping) at Level 3 is appropriate for floor supervisors, and the Level 4 NVQ is appropriate for head housekeepers. Some employers still ask for a BTEC qualification or the City & Guilds 708; the new NVQs in this area exceed the standards of the 708.

Some housekeepers who want to work towards the most senior positions study for the HCIMA Professional Certificate, or even the Professional Diploma.

How to find a job
Opportunities to train in housekeeping are advertised in the *Careers Guide* and *Handbook of Tourism*. However, if you are interested in this work you should write direct to hotel groups and privately owned hotels. These vacancies are advertised in the newspapers, trade magazines, and also handled by most hotel employment agencies.

Pay and conditions
A head housekeeper earns between £12,000 and £20,000 depending on the size of the hotel. Average pay for a floor housekeeper is £10,000 per year. Housekeeping staff must be prepared to work weekends, but start and finish work early; the usual day is from 7am to 3pm.

Where to find out more
The *Careers Guide* and *Handbook of Tourism*. The UK Housekeepers Association is the professional association for housekeepers.

Hotel room attendant

What you do
The day-to-day work of a room attendant includes making beds, changing linen, dusting, vacuuming, room presentation, and bathroom cleaning and hygiene.

Today, the job of room attendant carries more responsibility than in the past. Room attendants in many hotels are now completely responsible for the cleanliness, presentation and comfort of their own set of rooms. Most hotels have very high standards which must be followed exactly.

What you need

Formal qualifications are not essential, although many employers prefer those with some GCSEs. It is possible for those who start as room attendants to be promoted to floor housekeeper or even head housekeeper. An NVQ in Housekeeping is available. Level 1 is appropriate to room attendants. Level 2 (not yet available) will be for self-checking room attendants, Level 3 is for floor housekeepers/supervisors and Level 4 is for housekeepers.

Room attendants must be willing to work hard without supervision.

How to find a job

See newspaper advertisements. Some hotel employment agencies and Job Centres have vacancies. School leavers interested in this type of work should look at the training programmes offered by the Hotel and Catering Training Company (HCTC) or your local TEC.

Pay and conditions

Pay is usually in the region of £3.00 - £3.50 per hour. Most room attendants start early and finish early — a 7am to 3pm day is usual. Some jobs for room attendants are part time only (such as 8am-12 noon, five days a week).

Where to find out more

The *Careers Guide* and the *Handbook of Tourism*. Some hotel groups also have careers literature they will send you.

Case history

Claire White, age 19, London: Hotel room attendant

'I first started at the hotel about a year ago, when the job was advertised in the *Evening Standard*. At first, I thought the work would be just cleaning, but there is quite a bit more to it than that. At this hotel we all have 'our own' rooms which we're completely responsible for. There are rules which state to what standard everything must be cleaned and how it must be presented — from the making of the bed to the towels in the bathroom. We have to make sure these standards are followed exactly.

'This hotel has a very open promotion policy. If you work hard and are enthusiastic you can apply for promotion as vacancies come up, no matter what qualifications you have or haven't got. At the moment I'm working through the NVQs — and I'm quite keen about working my way up to floor housekeeper or even head housekeeper one day.'

Hotel cleaning staff

What you do
The work of the hotel cleaner is quite separate from that of the hotel room attendant. The cleaners service the public areas, such as lounges, bars and restaurants, offices, staff rooms and kitchens. This work involves the use of specialised cleaning equipment and materials and all work must be carried out to given standards, which are often set down in writing.

What you need
A pleasant personality and ability to work hard without supervision. Some previous experience of commercial cleaning (in an office, hospital etc) may be needed to get a job in a top hotel but it is not always essential.

How to find a job
These jobs are handled by Job Centres and hotel employment agencies, and also advertised in newspapers. It is also a good idea to 'phone or call into hotels to see if they have jobs available.

Pay and conditions
Hourly pay ranges between £3.00 and £6.00 per hour. The higher amounts are paid for work during the night and at weekends. Some cleaning jobs are part-time only.

Where to find out more
Contact hotels direct.

Linen room staff

What you do
The linen room is an essential part of any hotel. All sheets, blankets, towels and tablecloths for the bedrooms, bathrooms, restaurants and bars, plus staff uniforms, are issued from the linen room and are returned there after use. The linen room staff must ensure a continuous supply of clean linen; if they make a mistake the hotel cannot operate properly.

Some hotels have in-house laundries, although most use outside laundries to do all the washing and ironing. The linen room checks in soiled linen and despatches it to the laundry, checks the clean returns, then stores and issues fresh supplies.

Because the linen room operation is so important most large hotels have a linen room manager, several linen room supervisors and a team of linen room assistants.

What you need
Formal qualifications are not needed for linen room assistants. Those wishing to become linen room managers should have a GNVQ in Hospitality and Catering or appropriate NVQs. The NVQ in Catering and Hospitality (Housekeeping) is available at Levels 1, 3 and 4. Some employers still ask for a BTEC qualification or City & Guilds 708; the new NVQs in this area exceed the standards of the 708.

No experience is necessary. The larger hotel groups have training programmes for linen room staff.

How to find a job
Some hotel employment agencies and Job Centres have these vacancies. Otherwise see newspapers or contact hotel groups direct, especially if you want to work as a linen room manager or supervisor.

Pay and conditions
Pay starts at £3.50 per hour for linen room staff, up to £12,000 - £17,000 per year for a senior linen room manager. Linen room staff work mostly regular hours only (Monday to Friday 9am to 5pm), with occasional out of hours work.

Where to find out more
Contact the hotel groups direct. The UK Housekeepers Association is the professional association for staff working in this area.

Hotel sales and marketing staff

What you do
Sales and marketing staff are an essential part of the team, especially in the hotel groups. Very few guests walk in off the street — hotels have to be promoted to both private and business guests and the advantages of one hotel promoted vigorously over those of its competitors. Hotels also earn a good deal of their income from conferences and other special events and the sales and marketing staff must work hard to sell the services of the hotels they work for.

The sales and marketing staff devise a marketing strategy, plan and launch marketing campaigns, deal with the media and advertising agencies, and actively go out and sell to travel agents and corporate clients. Most hotel groups employ sales and marketing managers, marketing assistants, public relations executives and sales executives —

some of whom work as travelling representatives. This work may be carried out at individual hotels, and also at head office.

What you need
Many sales and marketing staff have a degree qualification. This need not be in Hotel and Catering. Once employed in the industry many sales and marketing staff study for the HCIMA or a sales and market- ing qualification, such as those offered by the Institute of Marketing (Certificate and Diploma in Marketing and Certificate in Sales Mar- keting). Those with thorough sales and marketing experience in another industry do not necessarily need any qualifications.

Sales and marketing staff must have a strong personality and be able to deal and negotiate with people at all levels.

How to find a job
Most of the large hotel groups have management training schemes which offer training in all aspects of hotel work and then allow suit- able people to specialise in sales and marketing, Write to them for details. Details of opportunities are also advertised in the *Careers Guide*, *Handbook of Tourism* and the advertising/marketing industry journals *Campaign* and *Marketing*.

Pay and conditions
Vary according to seniority and individual skills. Most managers earn £17-£24,000, together with a company car and product discounts. Some staff may be paid a commission on sales.

Where to find out more
Contact the hotel groups. Also see the *Careers Guide*, *Handbook of Tourism* and the ETB/BTA careers guides for graduates (see under 'Hotel Manager').

Case history

Sian Thomas, age 29, Surrey: Conference sales executive
'I'm not a graduate myself — although most of my colleagues are — and I came into the hospitality industry after learning about sales and marketing the practical way with a large financial services organisa- tion.

'My main role at the moment is to obtain bookings for the con- ference capacity of our group, which comprises 12 hotels, each of which is equipped with extensive conference and exhibition facilities. Conferences are a major revenue earner for the group and contribute about 30% of the takings in each hotel. Apart from anything else conference business is an excellent way of maintaining a good room occupancy rate. We also handle exhibitions and the bigger private parties, receptions etc.

'We have other people in the department who are responsible for generating leads. My job is then to go out and see them and try and persuade them to book their conference business with us. I might be negotiating with executives from a top Plc one day, and a trade union or political party the next day. They're all looking for whoever can host their conference most effectively, but at the most economical rate, and because there's such a lot of competition for this trade I'm often involved in some very tough and demanding negotiations.

'Although I'm basically a sales 'rep' I get quite excited about my work. It's very satisfying when, in just a few minutes, you can sign up a conference booking that will be worth £40,000 or £50,000 of business for one of your hotels. Once you get a satisfied customer they book with you again and again, and you get the credit for securing an awful lot of business. What don't I like? well, it's a very cutthroat business — even after weeks of negotiations your hard work can be wasted if one of your competitors comes in with a bid that's just a few pounds under yours!'

Conference/Banqueting/Exhibition organiser

What you do
Conferences, banquets, exhibitions and social events, such as wedding receptions, are important sources of income for many hotels. The larger ones have an organiser who will organise the entire event, co-ordinate the facilities provided by the various departments in the hotel (such as catering and accommodation) and be on hand at the event to ensure that everything runs smoothly.

What you need
Most employers will expect a BTEC HND or degree level qualification. This does not have to be in hotel and catering. Those with proven organisational ability in another industry may not require any formal qualifications.

Organisers must have a pleasant personality and a genuine aptitude for organisation.

How to find a job
As this type of position is quite specialist, vacancies come available only occasionally. See local and national newspapers and the *Caterer*

and Hotelkeeper journal. If you hold a HND or degree then contact the hotel groups who have a management training programme direct.

Pay and conditions
The average salary is in the region of £12-£20,000, depending on the size of the hotel. You may also be paid a commission if your work involves selling goods and services.

Where to find out more
Contact the hotel groups. Also see the *Careers Guide*, *Handbook of Tourism* and the ETB/BTA careers guides for graduates (see under 'Hotel Manager').

Hotel entertainment staff

What you do
Entertainment staff are employed in the larger hotels, and those in tourist resorts in the UK and abroad. They provide a programme of events. This might include floor shows, cabarets, parties, and special events for children. Some hotels also have leisure centres with swimming pools and other sports facilities.

The entertainment staff must usually think up ideas for entertainment, organise them, book acts, and run the events too. Although most hotels book professional musicians, singers and dancers, the entertainment staff are often expected to be able to perform too! The larger hotels may employ up to 10 entertainers, with an entertainments director in charge of them.

What you need
No formal qualifications are usually necessary. You must have a friendly, outgoing personality and it is an advantage to be able to speak a foreign language if you are hoping to work abroad. Leisure centre staff must in most cases have a recognised sports or teaching qualification.

Entertainment staff must have experience in a leisure environment. For example, a nightclub, sports centre, theatre or holiday centre. It is also an advantage if you can sing, dance, play an instrument, do DJ work or entertain children.

How to find a job
Very few positions of this type are advertised. Some are carried in *The Stage* newspaper and the *Overseas Jobs Express*. Theatrical/entertainment and hotel employment agencies also have vacancies; see

your *Yellow Pages*. Also contact hotels direct by 'phone, letter or in person.

Pay and conditions
Vary depending on experience. Many entertainers are employed on short summer contracts only.

Where to find out more
Further information about the opportunities in this type of work are given in *How to Get a Job in Travel and Tourism* (How To Books).

Hotel service and maintenance staff

What you do
Every hotel needs a wide range of service and maintenance staff. The work to be done by them includes stores work, plumbing, electrical, driving, DIY/small repairs, gardening and security. The extent to which this work is done by the hotel depends on the individual company; some companies hire contractors to do this work, whilst others hire their own staff.

What you need
Service and maintenance staff must have gained experience of the type of work they wish to do elsewhere. Hotels do not usually train their own service and maintenance staff and cannot usually employ the inexperienced. Trade qualifications (such as City & Guilds, or NVQs where these are available) are useful but not essential.

How to find a job
If you are interested in this type of work check newspaper advertisements and refer to Job Centres and private employment agencies.

Pay and conditions
Rates of pay for this type of work within hotels are the same as those for the same job in any other industry. Some out-of-hours work may be involved as much service and repair work is done at night.

Hotel personnel and training staff

What you do
Most hotels take personnel and training very seriously and the larger ones have their own personnel and training officers working at each

hotel, as well as at head office. Some companies, such as Forte, have their own staff training colleges.

The work of the personnel and training staff includes recruitment, employment law, welfare, organising and running training courses and administering the new system of National Vocational Qualifications (NVQs).

What you need
Most employers ask for a HND or degree qualification. These need not be in Hotel and Catering, but graduates in other disciplines should consider studying for the HCIMA Diploma after their degree. This will allow entry to a management/supervisory training course. Some employers will accept those with A levels or GNVQs. Those with substantial personnel/training experience in another industry may also be employed without a degree or HND.

A range of vocational qualifications from the Hotel and Catering Training Company are available to those employed in personnel/training. These include the Craft Trainer Award (CTA), Training Certificate and Training Diploma.

How to find a job
Contact the hotel groups directly. Also see advertisements in the national and local newspapers and trade publications such as *Caterer and Hotelkeeper* and *Personnel Management*.

Pay and conditions
Vary between £12-£20,000 depending on seniority, plus executive benefits. Personnel and training staff work mostly normal office hours only.

Where to find out more
The *Careers Guide* magazine; The Hotel and Catering Training Company; The Institute of Personnel Management; The Hotel and Catering Personnel and Training Association.

Hotel accountant

What you do
Hotel accounting and financial work has become an increasingly important area of the hospitality industry. Many companies remain profitable largely due to the skilful control and management of their money. The heads of several hotel groups, including Forte, are qualified accountants.

Hotel accountants, who work either at individual hotels or head office, will begin their careers by working in the areas of auditing, sales and purchase ledger, wages and salaries, costing and credit control.

What you need
Requirements vary according to the employer, from a degree or BTEC HND, to a GNVQ or A levels. These qualifications do not necessarily have to be in Accounting or Hotel and Catering. Those with experience in finance/accounts in another industry are often employed by the hospitality industry. Sometimes, those with experience in another area of hotel work are able to transfer into finance.

Many hotel accounts and finance employees study for a recognised accountancy qualification, or membership of the British Association of Hotel Accountants (BAHA).

How to find a job
See national newspapers and professional journals such as *Caterer and Hotelkeeper*, *Accountancy* and *Accountancy Magazine*. If you have a degree contact the hotel groups direct.

Pay and conditions
Varies according to qualifications, from £10,000 per year for a trainee, to £40,000 or much more, plus executive benefits, for a senior accountant or financial director.

Where to find out more
The British Association of Hotel Accountants (BAHA); the *Careers Guide*; contact the larger hotel groups.

JOBS IN CATERING

Catering unit manager

What you do
Unit manager is a hospitality industry term which can be used to describe the manager of a wide range of different catering establishments. This might be:

- A pub or wine bar.
- A fast-food takeaway: pizzas, burgers etc.
- A roadside catering operation (such as a motorway service area).
- An institutional kitchen (such as a school or hospital).

- A staff canteen or restaurant in an office or factory, or even an oil rig!
- An in-flight kitchen, preparing meals for aircraft.
- A snack bar in a shopping centre, or at a sports ground.
- An outside catering company, preparing food for wedding receptions etc.

In each case the unit manager is in overall charge of the operation. His or her work includes hiring, supervising and training staff, ordering supplies, budgeting, pricing, paying bills and customer care. The manager may even be involved with choosing the menu and working in the unit on a day to day basis. The responsibility compares with that of a restaurant manager, except that the environment, and so the customers and the type of food serviced, can vary a great deal — from smoked salmon for an in-flight meal on Concorde to steak pie and chips in a school or office canteen!

What you need
Qualifications required to become a unit manager vary from employer to employer. Some require a BTEC HND or degree in Hotel and Catering. Others will accept NVQs, A levels or a BTEC National qualification. This will get you a place on a management training scheme offered by the larger catering companies.

Some employers will accept people with appropriate NVQs only, or still ask for the previous City & Guilds 706 qualification. NVQs in Catering and Hospitality (Food Preparation and Cooking) are available at Levels 1-4. However, the 706 does not compare directly with the new NVQs.

Many companies will employ those without any formal qualifications if they have good previous experience in catering or have good management potential.

Potential managers in catering must be very hard-working, ambitious and able to get on well with both staff and customers.

Many would-be catering managers go on to obtain the HCIMA Professional Diploma, if appropriate.

How to find a job
The best way of finding a management training scheme is to write to the catering companies direct. Many addresses are given in this book and a large number of opportunities are advertised in the Caterer and Hotelkeeper *Careers Guide* magazine.

Apart from the well-known catering companies (such as McDonalds, Pizza Hut, Beefeater, Harvester, Welcome Break etc) many catering units are run by the specialist contract catering companies. The four largest in the UK are ARA, Compass, Gardner Merchant and Sutcliffe; some of these also have operations in other countries.

Pay and conditions
Vary according to experience and the takings of the unit you run. Most management trainees will start on £10-£13,000 per year. Shift work is usually involved.

Where to find out more
The *Careers Guide* and *Caterer and Hotelkeeper* both list many opportunities. The catering companies have careers literature which they will send you.

Catering section manager

What you do
Section managers are employed in the largest catering units to take charge of a section or department within the operation, under control of the unit manager. Jobs which fall into this category include assistant manager, restaurant manager, servery manager, kitchen manager, office manager and purchasing manager.

The job of section manager is a career position in its own right. Although some section managers eventually intend to become unit managers, many others intend to specialise in section management from the outset.

What you need
Most employers look for people with appropriate NVQs as a minimum. Some still ask for the previous City & Guilds 706 qualification. NVQs in Catering and Hospitality (Food Preparation and Cooking) are available at Levels 1-4. Someone holding an NVQ at Level 2 will have similar skills to someone holding a 706 Part 1, although both systems are organised differently. Many would-be managers entering at this level have training or experience as chefs or cooks.

Some companies will employ those without any formal qualifications if they have good previous experience in catering or have good management potential. For example, waiters and kitchen staff with good potential can often obtain promotion to these positions.

How to find a job
These jobs are advertised in newspapers and in some Job Centres. Also write to the catering companies direct. Many addresses are given

in this book and a large number of opportunities are advertised in the Caterer and Hotelkeeper *Careers Guide* magazine.

Pay and conditions
Vary according to the individual position and your experience, but pay averages £8-£12,000. Shift work is usually involved.

Where to find out more
The *Careers Guide* and *Caterer and Hotelkeeper* both list many opportunities. The catering companies produce careers literature which they will send you.

Catering executive manager

What you do
The executive manager is employed by the larger catering companies only. The job is to manage the catering company rather than run an individual unit. Executive managers work mostly at a head or area office.

Areas which an executive manager may be responsible for include negotiating catering contracts, sales and marketing, finance and personnel. Many executive managers are area managers, in charge of catering units in a particular region.

What you need
Executive managers must usually have a BTEC HND qualification as a minimum. Some require a degree. This can be in Hospitality and Catering or a business discipline. Many executive managers start their careers as, or are promoted from, unit managers; in this case it is possible to start with other BTEC, City & Guilds or appropriate NVQs only.

Some executive managers study for further professional qualifications. These include vocational qualifications such as the HCIMA Diploma or Institute of Management qualifications.

How to find a job
The largest catering companies have training programmes for graduates and others aiming for executive positions. These jobs are rarely advertised and it is best to write to suitable companies for further details.

Pay and conditions
These depend on the position and the responsibility involved, but pay averages £18-£24,000. Such jobs are also likely to include executive

benefits including company car and, with some companies, the opportunity to work abroad.

Where to find out more
Contact the catering companies direct. The British Tourist Authority (BTA) booklet *Graduates in Tourism and Leisure* provides useful information for graduates on this type of work.

Restaurant manager

What you do
The restaurant manager, whether in a hotel or a stand-alone restaurant, is responsible for the smooth running of the establishment. His or her duties include supervising and training the waiters, liaising with the head chef, monitoring the reservations system and ensuring that the service in the restaurant is professional and efficient. Some restaurant managers are involved with menu planning, marketing and ensuring profitability of the operation.

A restaurant manager often starts his or her career as a waiter, member of the kitchen staff, restaurant supervisor or assistant restaurant manager, and then is promoted on merit.

What you need
Many restaurant managers have training or experience as chefs or waiters. Most employers look for those with appropriate NVQs; some still ask for the previous City and Guilds 706 (food preparation) or 707 (food service) qualifications. NVQs in Catering and Hospitality in either Food Preparation and Cooking, or Serving Food and Drink/ Food Service, are available at Levels 1-4. Would-be restaurant managers should have achieved Level 3 minimum, preferably Level 4 in one of these fields.

Restaurant managers must be efficient, well organised and polite and be able to get on well with staff and customers. Knowledge of a foreign language is useful for some top jobs.

How to find a job
See advertisements in national and local newspapers. Some catering employment agencies also have these jobs. Also make contact with hotels and restaurant owners — many jobs are obtained by word of mouth.

Pay and conditions
Vary from around £12,000 to £17,000. Many restaurant managers re-

ceive a small basic wage but also get tips, or a share in the profits of the restaurant. You will have to work shifts, late nights and weekends.

Where to find out more
Contact restaurants direct. The *Careers Guide* and *Handbook of Tourism* also provide further information.

Waiter

What you do
The waiter is a key member of the team in any restaurant, bar or hotel. A good waiter does not merely serve food and drink, but does it efficiently, professionally and pleasantly. Although, in the UK, waiting was often regarded as a casual job, it is now coming to be regarded as a career. This has been the case in most European countries for many years.

A career in waiting is open to all but there are still only a small number of waitresses in top restaurants.

There are various types of waiter:

● **Head restaurant waiter**: The head waiter is in overall charge of the waiting team and directs and supervises the table service. He or she is also responsible for ensuring the customers are satisfied. The head waiter may also be called on to serve important guests, or more demanding dishes, such as flambé dishes which are cooked at the table. Large restaurants may also have assistant head waiters.

● **Restaurant waiter**: The duties of a waiter include table presentation, taking orders, recommending dishes and table clearing as well as food service. In a good quality restaurant the waiters usually work in pairs, with a waiter, who is a senior member of the team, being assisted by a commis (junior) waiter. The term *chef de rang* is used for waiters in top restaurants.

● **Wine waiter**: Wine waiters (also known as *sommeliers*) are employed in top class restaurants to provide the wine service. This includes recommending wines, taking orders and serving. Wine waiters may also be involved in purchasing the wine and keeping the restaurant's wine cellar.

● **Bar waiter**: The bar waiter (also known as a cocktail waiter) is employed in hotels and some restaurants. Their job is to take orders for and serve drinks at the table in the lounge or bar. A bar waiter would not usually be involved in food service but would have a specialist knowledge of alcoholic and non-alcoholic beverages.

● **Room service waiter:** Room service waiters are usually employed in hotels of minimum three-star rating and higher. The work involves taking orders for, presenting and serving drinks and food in guests' rooms, and may involve simple food preparation and cooking.

What you need

All waiters must have a pleasant, service orientated personality and a good appearance.

Formal qualifications are not usually needed for any of these jobs, although many employers like to see four good GCSEs. Those aiming for more senior positions (like head waiter or restaurant manager) should have the appropriate NVQs, and some may even wish to take a GNVQ course although this is not essential.

Catering and Hospitality NVQs appropriate to this work are:

Level 1: Serving food and drink — bar.
Serving food and drink — table/tray.

Level 2: Serving food and drink — restaurant. (Includes silver service as an optional unit; essential for those hoping to work in a good quality restaurant.)
Serving food and drink — bar.

Level 3: Food and drink service — on licensed premises supervisory management.

Some employers may still ask for the old City & Guilds 707 qualification. Someone holding an NVQ at Level 2 will have most of the skills required of someone holding a 707 Part 1 and 2 and someone holding an NVQ at Level 3 will have them all.

It is possible for people without qualifications to be taken on by good quality restaurants if they have experience in a smaller restaurant, and a flair for this type of work.

A range of further qualifications can be obtained by those working in waiting. These include those offered by the Academy of Wine Service.

How to find a job
School leavers interested in this type of work should look at the training programmes offered by the Hotel and Catering Training Company (HCTC) or your local TEC. Many colleges offering NVQ courses are able to introduce their students to employers which may lead to the offer of a job. Also see local newspaper advertisements and consider contacting restaurants in your area either by letter, telephone or in person.

Pay and conditions
Wages range from £3.17 per hour minimum to £12-£14,000 per year for an experienced waiter in a good hotel or restaurant.

Where to find out more
The *Careers Guide* and the *Handbook of Tourism* provide further information. The large hotel groups also have careers literature. The Academy of Wine Service provides training courses.

Case history

Michael Derbyshire, age 22, Berkshire: Restaurant waiter
'I never set out to become a waiter, but of the different choices I looked at after leaving school it appealed to me because it's obviously not a 9-5 job. I started out on a local training scheme which my school careers teacher found out about for me. It involved studying at college — I took the City & Guilds 707 as it was then — and work experience in a local restaurant. In the summer holidays I also worked as a waiter in a restaurant in Tenerife!

'I found my first job through the college. It was in the restaurant of a large, local hotel. This is quite a good way to start because the atmosphere is a lot less formal than some restaurants, and there are plenty of old hands who are willing to help you out. There's quite a bit of difference between just serving food and doing it in an efficient and professional way, but I soon found it was something I can do well. Not everybody is comfortable about serving others — you've got to separate the way you deal with people privately and professionally.

'After two years I moved to my present job which is in a very upmarket, privately owned restaurant. We only have 40 covers and a very small team providing a very high standard of service to our diners — most of whom are regulars and spend £150-£200 on a meal for four. At this level you've got to be on the ball all the time. The tips are usually very, very good and make quite a big difference to our basic wage.

'I've now decided that I want to stay in waiting, and I've every intention of making it to assistant or head waiter sometime in the future. If there's one thing I do regret it's that your own social life is disrupted — sometimes we don't finish here until 12.30 or even 1am!

Bar staff

What you do
Bar staff prepare and dispense drinks in hotels and restaurants, pubs, wine bars, nightclubs, private clubs and more out-of-the-ordinary situations, such as at airports or on cruise ships.

The amount of skill and knowledge required varies considerably depending on the type of work. Whilst little knowledge is needed for a part-time job in a pub, professional bar staff in a top hotel, for example, need extensive knowledge of wines and spirits, cocktails, serving techniques, customer service, stock control and cash handling, plus health and licensing regulations.

What you need
Bar staff must have a pleasant personality and good experience. Those wishing to work in a top hotel will find it easier to get a job if they have some previous experience of bar work in a pub or smaller hotel.

Formal qualifications are not usually necessary. Those with the appropriate NVQs will find it easier to get a job. The NVQs appropriate to bar staff are the same as those for waiters (see previous section for further details). Those hoping to progress to the job of bar manager in a large establishment may find it an advantage to have a GNVQ (or BTEC National qualification for those who already hold one).

A range of further qualifications is available to those planning to develop a career in bar work and progress to the job of bar manager. These are offered by the Hotel and Catering Training Company and others, such as the Academy of Wine Service.

How to find a job
This type of work is advertised in local newspapers and also available through Job Centres and hotel/catering employment agencies. You should also make a direct approach to establishments where bars are operated, such as hotels, restaurants, pubs and wine bars. Some bars, such as those at airports, are operated by the contract catering companies.

Most new bar staff start as commis bar staff before progressing to bar staff and then head bar staff or bar manager if suitable.

Pay and conditions
From £3.83 per hour up to £10-£12,000 per year. Shift work is usually involved.

Where to find out more
The *Careers Guide*. Professional associations involved with this type of work include the Academy of Wine Service, Wine and Spirit Education Trust, United Kingdom Bartenders Guild and the British Institute of Innkeeping.

Chef

What you do
Food preparation is the main type of work in the catering industry. Other than this the work is very varied. Your work might involve working in an exclusive restaurant, or a simple bistro or pub — doing anything from cooking a hamburger to the most elaborate French dish.

Chefs in most establishments work according to a strictly set down hierarchy, each with their own individual duties and responsibilities:

- **Head chef**: The head chef runs the kitchen and liaises with the restaurant manager and the hotel manager, if the establishment is in a hotel. Duties include menu planning, staff supervision and training and possibly also finance and budgeting, with only a limited amount of time available for cooking. Few head chefs have less than 10 years' experience and usually have much more before reaching this position.

- **Sous chef**: The sous chefs are deputy chefs and have an important supervisory and management role, as well as doing some of the cooking. Large kitchens have a senior sous chefs, sous chefs and junior sous chefs. A chef requires, on average, at least five years' experience (including two as a chef de partie) before they are able to seek promotion to the job of sous chef.

- **Chef de partie**: The chefs de partie do the bulk of the cooking in every kitchen. Under the partie system each chef de partie specialises in cooking a particular part of the meal. For example:

  Chef Entremetier: Vegetables
  Chef Rôtisseur: Roasting
  Chef Poissonier: Fish
  Chef Saucier: Entrées
  Chef Pâtissier: Desserts

- **Commis chef**: The commis chefs are junior chefs and work under the direction of the chefs de partie, usually preparing and cooking the less elaborate dishes. A chef will usually need to have at least three years' experience as a commis chef (including one year as a demi chef) before moving on to become a chef de partie.

- **Trainee chef**: The trainee chef is the most junior member of the team and works in all areas of the kitchen under supervision. Most chefs spend three years as trainee chefs before moving up to the position of commis chef.

School leavers usually start as trainee chefs, but college leavers usually start as commis chefs.

What you need
School leavers need no minimum academic qualifications to become a trainee chef, but most employers like to see four GCSEs.

If you want to train at college you will need to satisfy the entry requirements for that college, which will depend on the individual course and college in question. You should check with the college to find out what these are.

A large number of colleges offer courses leading to NVQs in Food Preparation and Cooking at Levels 1-4. Some employers still ask for the previous City and Guilds 706 qualification. The new NVQs are organised very differently to the 706 qualification but someone holding an NVQ in Food Preparation and Cooking at Level 2 will have broadly the same skills as someone holding a 706 Part 1 qualification.

How to find a job
- **School leavers**: If you want to take up a job straight after leaving school you should look at the training programmes offered by the Hotel and Catering Training Company (HCTC) or your local TEC. Also consider contacting your local hotels and restaurants directly and asking if they have any positions available for trainee chefs. You will then undergo three years of on-the-job training, and possibly some day-release study at college, before becoming a commis chef.

- **College leavers**: If you wish to study at catering college then, on completion of your course, you can apply for the job of commis chef. Colleges have good contacts with employers. These jobs are also advertised in newspapers and handled by hotel and catering employment agencies. You should also contact local hotels and restaurants direct.

All new chefs start as a trainee or commis chef and work their way up the hierarchy.

Pay and conditions
£6-£10,000 per year for a trainee or commis chef. £12-£28,000 for other chefs. All these depend on experience, ability and size of the establishment. The top head chefs can command salaries of £60,000 or more.

Where to find out more
The Caterer and Hotelkeeper *Career Guide* and the *Handbook of Tourism* give further details. The large hotel groups have careers literature. Professional associations for this type of work include the Chefs and Cooks Circle and the Cookery and Food Association.

Case history

Ellen Chapman, age 23, Wales: Chef de partie
'I've wanted to be a chef since I was 12 or 13 and as soon as I was old enough took a part-time job helping out in the kitchens at a local restaurant. The chefs there were very helpful but I'm sure they thought that chopping and cleaning was as far as a woman should go in the kitchen — there's still quite a lot of prejudice and very few women chefs.

'I didn't go to college straight after leaving school, but did a year working full-time in the restaurant. I didn't have to, but it helped me make sure the work was for me, and helped me save up some money. At college I took the City & Guilds 706 Part 1 and 2 qualifications.

'My first job after college was in a smart hotel in Cardiff. Although by then you're a fully qualified chef there's still a fair bit to learn about — especially how to handle the pressure of a full dining room, with half the kitchen staff off sick, at one o'clock on a Sunday lunchtime. I've worked my way up to chef de partie, moving over to this hotel when my head chef gained a promotion and asked some of us to go with him, which was very satisfying.

'At the moment I've got my sights firmly set on the job of head chef one day. But I'm not expecting it to be easy, especially as a woman. If, one day, I can afford it then I would seriously think about buying or starting my own restaurant or small hotel.'

Kitchen porter/Kitchen assistant

What you do
Kitchen porters and assistants are essential in any commercial kitchen.

A TYPICAL CAREER PATH FOR A CHEF

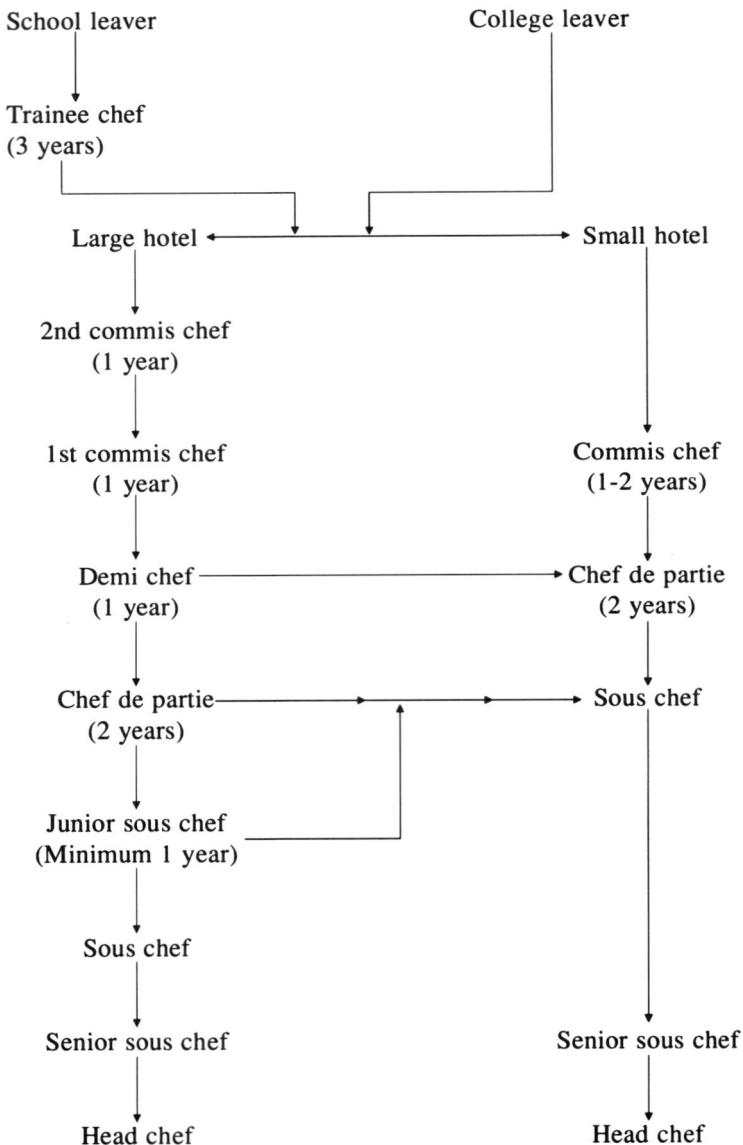

School leaver   College leaver

Trainee chef
(3 years)

Large hotel ←→ Small hotel

2nd commis chef
(1 year)

1st commis chef   Commis chef
(1 year)   (1-2 years)

Demi chef ————→ Chef de partie
(1 year)   (2 years)

Chef de partie ————→ Sous chef
(2 years)

Junior sous chef
(Minimum 1 year)

Sous chef

Senior sous chef   Senior sous chef

Head chef   Head chef

(With thanks to Hilton UK for providing this example.)

Their work is not only portering but also includes receiving deliveries, keeping the stores, delivering food and equipment around the kitchen and cleaning/hygiene procedures. Kitchen porters may also be called on to do basic food preparation, keep records and attend to basic paperwork.

What you need
No formal qualifications are required. Kitchen porters must be physically fit and hard working. For suitable people there may be opportunities to obtain NVQs and gain promotion to other jobs around a hotel or restaurant.

How to find a job
Jobs are advertised in newspapers, Job Centres and are handled by hotel/catering employment agencies. Also approach hotels and restaurants direct.

Pay and conditions
Around £3.00 per hour. Shift work is usually involved.

Where to find out more
Contact hotels and restaurants direct.

Details of opportunities for waiters, bar staff and chefs aboard cruise ships are given in *How to Get a Job in Travel and Tourism*, also published by How To Books.

Cook

What you do
The work of a cook is similar to that of chef, but usually involves a more basic level of cooking; cooks are usually found working in institutional kitchens, such as schools and hospitals, and contract catering, rather than hotels and restaurants. The job involves various types of work including fast food cook and short order cook: a cook who prepares small quantities of dishes which are supplementary to the main menu.

What you need
Formal qualifications are not needed to start as a trainee, although some experience in a small commercial kitchen (such as a pub etc) would be useful. Those hoping to obtain more senior jobs within the industry should consider taking a college course to obtain the appropriate NVQs.

NVQs in Food Preparation and Cooking — General, and Food Preparation and Cooking — Quick Service, are available at Level 1. These are appropriate to the job of fast food cook. NVQs in Food Preparation and Cooking are available at Level 2. These are appropriate to the job of cook and are a similar (but not identical) qualification to the previous City and Guilds 706 Part 1 qualification which some employers will refer to.

How to find a job
Refer to advertisements in newspapers. Contact the contract catering companies direct. Many opportunities are advertised in the *Careers Guide*.

Pay and conditions
Average £10-£14,000 per year — the higher figure for a senior cook in a large contract catering unit. Working hours will depend on the type of catering unit in which you work.

Where to find out more
Refer to the *Careers Guide*. Some of the contract catering companies issue careers literature.

Catering assistant

What you do
The catering assistant works, not in a hotel or restaurant, but in an institutional or contract catering situation or similar. This might include a school or a hospital, a fast food outlet or a motorway service station. A catering assistant assists the cooks or chefs and carries out many of the duties of a kitchen assistant in a hotel. However, a catering assistant also does basic food preparation and cooking. This will include making sandwiches, pastries and desserts, salads and drinks.

What you need
Academic qualifications are not needed to start as a trainee, although some experience in a small commercial kitchen (such as a pub etc) would be useful. NVQs in Food Preparation and Cooking — General, and Food Preparation and Cooking — Quick Service, are available at Level 1. These are appropriate to the job of catering assistant.
    Some catering companies will employ people with four GCSEs, or a GNVQ, or a BTEC National qualification (for those who already have one), or NVQs in Food Preparation and Cooking at Level 3 or 4

to start as a catering assistant with a view to working their way up to become a catering unit manager.

How to find a job
Refer to advertisements in newspapers. Job Centres and hotel/catering employment agencies also handle these jobs. Contact the contract catering companies direct. Many opportunities are advertised in the *Careers Guide*.

Pay and conditions
£3.00 - £3.50 per hour. Working hours will depend on the type of catering unit.

Where to find out more
Refer to the *Careers Guide*.

Counter food service assistant

What you do
Counter assistants work wherever food is offered self-service. This might be in an office, school or factory canteen, although the main areas for this type of work today are in fast food outlets and the free-flow restaurants, such as you might find at a motorway service area. The work includes serving customers, stocking the displays, and basic food preparation.

What you need
Academic qualifications are not essential. An NVQ in Food Preparation and Cooking — Quick Service is available at Level 1 and is appropriate to the job of counter service assistant.

Some catering companies will employ people with four GCSEs, or a GNVQ, or a BTEC National qualification (for those who already have one), or NVQs in Food Preparation and Cooking at Level 3 or 4 to start as a counter assistant with a view to working their way up to become a catering unit manager.

Counter service assistants should have a pleasant, service-minded personality.

How to find a job
Refer to advertisements in newspapers. Job Centres and hotel/catering employment agencies also handle these jobs. Contact the contract catering companies direct. Many opportunities are advertised in the *Careers Guide*.

Pay and conditions
£3.00-£3.50 per hour. Working hours will depend on the type of catering unit.

Where to find out more
Refer to the *Careers Guide.*

Cashier

What you do
Cashiers work in restaurants and other catering locations, such as self-service cafes. The work includes use of a cash register, making up and issuing bills, receiving cash, cheque and credit card payments or, in a hotel, charging meals to guests' room accounts.

What you need
Cashiers must be able to work quickly and accurately and be good with figures. Applicants with four GCSEs will have an advantage. To work in a top restaurant some experience in cashier work, such as in a shop, would be an advantage. Cashiers must have a pleasant personality.

How to find a job
Refer to advertisements in newspapers. Job Centres and hotel/catering employment agencies also handle these jobs.

Pay and conditions
£3.00-£3.50 per hour. Working hours will depend on the type of location.

Where to find out more
Refer to the *Careers Guide.*

● **Tip**: Qualifications in use in England, Wales and Northern Ireland have been used in this chapter. In all cases the equivalent Scottish qualifications (SCEs, SVQs, GSVQs and SCOTVEC) are also acceptable.

● **Tip**: To avoid repetition the male equivalents of job titles have been used in this chapter. For example, Manager and Waiter. However, all these jobs are available to both women and men.

4
How and Where to Find a Job

HOW TO USE UK NEWSPAPERS TO FIND JOBS

A large number of vacancies in hotel and catering work are advertised in the main daily newspapers.

Each newspaper does not carry a large number of vacancies but, when all the newspapers are looked at together, there is a reasonable number each week. It is unlikely to be worth buying all the newspapers every week; most main libraries will have them in their reading room.

The following national newspapers mostly carry vacancies for management jobs:

— *Daily Telegraph*
— *Sunday Telegraph*
— *Daily Mail*
— *Daily Express*
— *The Mail on Sunday*
— *Sunday Express*
— *The Independent*
— *The Guardian*
— *The Times*
— *The Independent on Sunday*
— *The Sunday Times*

Also look at your regional, local and free newspapers, although the number of vacancies will depend on whether there are many hotel and catering employers in your area. London's *Evening Standard* carries a large number of hotel and catering job vacancies; Tuesday and Friday are the main days for them to appear.

Local, regional and free newspapers carry advertisements for all types of jobs, not just management.

USING FOREIGN NEWSPAPERS TO FIND JOBS

If you want to find a job abroad then it is a good idea to use foreign newspapers for this purpose. As in the UK most foreign newspapers carry job advertisements. You would need to speak the language of that country in order to understand the ads, although some countries, such as Spain and Greece, do have a few English language newspapers.

Where to get them
It is not always necessary to travel abroad to buy foreign newspapers. They are available from these sources in the UK:

● Newsagents in major cities: however, the cover prices are high.

● Libraries in major cities: some libraries have a limited selection of foreign newspapers.

● Foreign Embassies and Consulates: the UK Embassies of some foreign countries have reading rooms where you can consult their newspapers.

● On subscription. It is possible to have foreign newspapers posted to you on a daily basis, although the cost is high. This can be arranged through an agency such as Collets Subscription Service, Denington Estate, Wellingborough, Northants NN8 2QT. Tel: (01933) 224351.

Details of the main newspapers in various countries around the world are given in Chapter 6.

HOTEL AND CATERING TRADE PUBLICATIONS TO READ

There are a number of monthly and weekly trade publications which can be used to locate job vacancies both in the UK and abroad. Many of the vacancies they carry are for experienced people, but it may still be useful to read these publications.

Trade publications can be purchased on subscription or read free of charge in the periodicals department of your local large town or city library. These publications are particularly useful:

● *British Hotelier*

- *Caterer and Hotelkeeper*
- *Catering Management*
- *Hospitality*
- *Hotel and Guest House*
- *Hotel and Restaurant Magazine*
- *Leisure Opportunities*
- *Leisure Week*
- *Local Authority Week*
- *Morning Advertiser* (The Society of Licensed Victuallers)
- *Restaurant Business*
- *Scottish Licensed Trade Guardian*
- *The Publican*
- *Overseas Jobs Express.* This fortnightly newspaper carries some job vacancies in hotels and catering, including casual and seasonal jobs and full time vacancies. It is available on subscription from: Overseas Jobs Express, Premier House, Shoreham Airport, Sussex BN43 5FF.

Other periodicals

You should also read:

- *Careers Guide.* This is published annually by the *Caterer and Hotelkeeper* — the hospitality industry's major weekly trade journal — in association with the Hotel and Catering Training Company. In addition to much useful information on working in the industry it contains job advertising and advertisements for training schemes, including management and graduate training schemes. Available from: Caterer and Hotelkeeper, Quadrant House, The Quadrant, Sutton, Surrey SM2 5AS. Tel: (0181) 652 3500.

- *Handbook of Tourism* (HOT). This is published bi-annually and contains advertisements for training schemes, including management and graduate training schemes. Available at libraries.

- *HCIMA Reference Book.* This is published by the Hotel, Catering and Institutional Management Association and contains advertisements for training schemes, including management and graduate training schemes. Available at libraries.

USING THE EMPLOYMENT SERVICE

The UK employment service

It is possible to use the UK Employment Service to get a job both in the UK and some other countries. These are mostly countries which are members of the European Union: Belgium, Denmark, Ireland, France, Germany, Greece, Italy, Luxembourg, Netherlands, Portugal and Spain.

To obtain details of these jobs visit your local Job Centre and ask for details of any vacancies in hotel and catering fields. If you are interested in jobs abroad ask for details of jobs available through the **Overseas Placing Unit** (OPU). These are usually jobs that government-run employment services in other countries have had difficulty filling; so they have asked the services in other countries to try and fill them.

If no suitable vacancies are available then fill in a form ES13 at the Job Centre. When you do this your details will be held on file and you will be contacted if any suitable vacancies arise through the OPU within the next six months.

The main limitation with this system is that most of the jobs that become available are for qualified and experienced people who speak a foreign language. If you are not already qualified and experienced the chances of finding a job may be small.

Some of the OPU's vacancies are also listed on the ES Jobfinder Service which is available on Channel 4 Teletext, page 649.

How to use the job centres in foreign countries

Every foreign country has a government-run employment service very much like British Job Centres and, in many cases, it is possible for people from the UK to use this service to get a job.

UK nationals are legally entitled to use state employment services in all the European Union countries. You have a right to be treated equally with nationals of that country. However, remember that many of the jobs these services have will require qualifications, experience and knowledge of a foreign language. There will also usually be a lot of competition from people who already live in that country for these jobs.

To use the state employment service in other countries you must usually visit them in person. They do not usually deal with telephone calls or letters from abroad. Some useful contacts are given in Chapter 6.

USING PRIVATE EMPLOYMENT AGENCIES

Employment agencies in the UK

One way of finding the job you want is to register with a privately run employment agency. They will take your details and try and find you a job with an employer who has notified them of a vacancy. The main limitation with this method is that most of the jobs are for qualified and experienced people. Employment agencies may not have many jobs suitable for school and college leavers. Most of the jobs handled by agencies will be in the UK, although they do sometimes have jobs in other countries of the world too.

Details of employment agencies in your area can be found in your local *Yellow Pages* under the heading 'Employment Agencies and Consultants'. Details of many more agencies throughout the UK can be found in a book called the *FRES Yearbook* which will be in many libraries.

Most employment agencies handle all types of jobs. A few specialise in hotel and catering staff. Some of these are:

Abbey Recruitment, 18 James Street, London W1M 5HN. Tel: (0171) 495 4342.

AGS Personnel, Eden House, 120 Eastgate, Pickering, North Yorks YO18 7DW. Tel: (01751) 472289.

Alfred Marks Catering, 170 Fleet Street, London EC4 2EA. Tel: (0171) 248 4281.

Ashdown Catering Appointments, 21 Monson Road, Tunbridge Wells, Kent TN1 1LS. Tel: (01892) 517977.

Berkeley Scott Personnel Consultants, Berkeley House, 11 Ockford Road, Godalming, Surrey GU7 1QU. Tel: (01483) 414141.

Blue Arrow Personnel Services, 83 Camp Road, St Albans, Herts AL1 5US. Tel: (01727) 866266.

Christopher's Personnel, London House, 19 Old Court Place, London W8 4PL. Tel: (0171) 937 8314.

Classic Recruitment, 811 High Road, London N12 8JW. Tel: (0181) 446 8224.

Cooke & Mellor Recruitment, Clayton Business Park, Blackburn Road, Clayton le Moors, Accrington, Lancashire BB5 5JW. Tel: (01254) 393988.

Catering Recruitment and Consultancy, 70 High Street, Honiton, Devon EX14 8PD. Tel: (01404) 47733.

KPC Recruitment Agency, 16 Green Acres, Welwyn Garden City, Herts AL7 4LJ. Tel: (01707) 375403.

Mayday Staff Services, 2 Shoreditch High Street, London E1. Tel: (0171) 377 1352.

Paterson Recruitment, 2 Littlegate Street, Oxford OX1 1QT. Tel: (01865) 790100.

Paul Powell, 63 The Row, Sutton, Ely, Cambs CB6 2PB. Tel: (01353) 777991.

Reed Catering, 183 Victoria Street, London SW1E 5NE. Tel: (0171) 828 1233.

Roche Personnel, 1 Dover Street, Cambridge CB1 1DY. Tel: (01223) 302759.

Top Flight Recruitment, 319a Holdenhurst Road, Bournemouth BH8 8BT. Tel: (01202) 300469.

Towngate Personnel, 65 Seamoor Road, Bournemouth BH4 9AE. Tel: (01202) 752955.

Employment agencies in the UK are not allowed to charge the employee a fee. This may not apply in other countries.

Using employment agencies in other countries

If you wish to work abroad you should consider using private employment agencies in the country of your choice. These are usually willing to help people from other countries, especially if you have a particular skill to offer and speak the local language.

Private employment agencies can be found in most foreign countries, although in a few (such as Germany) they are prohibited by law. Some useful contacts are given in Chapter 6.

The best way to find out if an employment agency may be able to find you a job is to put together a letter and CV (curriculum vitae) telling them about yourself and what you can do and then post it off to all the agencies you can find.

GETTING A JOB BY WRITING LETTERS

Only a proportion of jobs in any industry are found by actually looking for vacancies that are advertised in newspapers, trade publications and through agencies. A significant number are obtained by what is known as speculative application. This means that you actually approach potential employers and offer your services, rather than wait for them to advertise. The chances of being offered a job by doing this are greater than many people realise.

For example, some hotel groups very rarely advertise their vacancies for staff and never advertise their management or graduate training schemes. They find it unnecessary because so many people contact them asking about the possibility of work.

If you want to use this method then prepare a letter which tells a would-be employer about yourself and what you feel you can offer them. Also put together a CV (curriculum vitae) which gives your personal details, details of your education and details of any work experience you have had. Send these to all the employers you can find out about, who you feel will have jobs of the type you want. For example, if you would like to become a hotel manager send a letter and CV to both the large hotel groups and smaller, individually owned hotels.

Addresses of possible employers can be obtained from:

● The *Yellow Pages*. Directories for all the UK and many foreign countries are available in most major libraries.

● *The Kompass Directories*. This is a very detailed directory listing almost all the companies in most of the countries of the world. A separate directory is published for each country. These directories are kept by most major libraries.

● The *HCIMA Reference Book*
● The *Handbook of Tourism*
● The *World Hotel Directory*
These publications list hotel and catering companies throughout the UK, and worldwide. They are available at most major libraries.

● Tourist offices. Offices in the UK and other countries can often supply addresses of possible employers, especially hotels.

● Chambers of Commerce. Chambers of commerce in many foreign countries can supply details of their members, especially hotels and large catering companies.

Many of the main companies in hotels and catering in the UK and worldwide are listed later in this book.

Some examples of letters and CVs are given later.

GETTING A JOB BY PERSONAL CALLING

The method discussed above can be a very effective way of finding out about jobs. However, in some situations it can be quicker and easier to contact possible employers by telephone or in person, rather than writing them a letter and hoping they will reply.

This method is particularly suitable if you are looking for casual work abroad. For example, in some towns and resorts you may find that a hotel or restaurant only advertises jobs by simply placing a 'Help Wanted' sign in their window, or by waiting for people to walk in and ask for work. This is very common in some foreign countries.

● **Firstly**
Find out the cost of travelling to the particular country you wish to work in, and staying there, while you look for a job. In some countries food and accommodation is more expensive than in the UK. It is a good idea to buy a ticket for your return journey before you travel out so that you can return home easily if no work is available.

● **Secondly**
Find out if you need any permits or visas in order to travel to the country and look for work. This is covered in Chapter 2 and Chapter 6 and you can also find out by asking the Embassy or Consulate of the relevant country. Addresses for these are given in Chapter 6.

● **Thirdly**
Make a list of possible employers before you leave the UK. This can be done by using the sources listed in the previous section.

● **Finally**
When you arrive abroad decide what you are going to do and say before you set out to see potential employers. Take a copy of your CV and any qualifications you hold. Ask to see the manager or personnel manager. As well as asking them for a job be sure to tell them what you think you can offer them and their hotel, restaurant, cafe or bar.

OTHER SOURCES OF JOBS TO USE

Springboard

Springboard is an organisation which has been set up to promote the hotel, catering, leisure and tourism industries as a career. It is sponsored by some of the large companies who operate in the hospitality industry.

Springboard offers advice on training, qualifications, careers and job vacancies. Its services are available to people of all ages, including young people thinking about a career in hospitality and older people making a career change.

At the moment Springboard operates only in the Greater London area, but may operate nationally in the future. It is open for letter and telephone enquiries and to personal callers at 1 Denmark Street, London WC2H 8LP. Tel: (0171) 497 8654.

The Hotel and Catering Training Company

The HCTC can offer training and work experience, possibly leading to employment, for 16-17 year old school leavers. Further details of this scheme are given in Chapter 2.

SAMPLE LETTERS AND CVs

The following pages offer some sample enquiry and application letters and a model CV.

Tips on presenting letters and CVs

- A CV must always be typed and should fit on one side of one piece of A4 paper only.

- Letters may be handwritten or typed. If you write make sure your writing is neat and readable.

- Use good quality white or blue writing paper and write in black or blue only. Do not write letters on lined paper, or in red ink or pencil.

- Never send out a letter or CV containing any mistakes or corrections.

- After you have written your letter and CV get a friend to read it through to make sure it is clear.

- If you are applying for a job abroad, then the foreign language headings shown in the model CV (page 83) will be of help to the employer.

The ABC Employment Agency
1 Sussex Road,
Anytown.
Sussex BN1 1AA

David Davidson,
1 The Road,
Anytown,
Sussex BN1 1AA
Tel: 0123 999999
1 July 199X

Dear Sirs,

I am writing to enquire as to whether you might have any vacancies in the hotel industry for which I might be suitable.

I am 22 years old and very interested in obtaining a job as a hotel manager/trainee manager.

At the moment I work in a motor dealership here in Anytown. I have four years' experience in our service reception and customer services departments. Although I do not have any previous experience of working in a hotel, I do feel that my experience of working with and serving the public would be of great value in hotel work.

I enclose my curriculum vitae which gives some more details about my qualifications and experience. If you have any vacancies for which I might be suitable then please do contact me at any time.

Yours faithfully,

David Davidson.

Enclosed: CV.

Fig 4(a). A letter to an employment agency enquiring about suitable vacancies.

The Manager,   Jane Jones,
Hotel Americas Group,   20 The Road,
Playa de Las Americas,   Anytown,
Tenerife,   Sussex BN1 1AA
Spain.   England.
                                  Tel: +44 0123 999999
                                           1 July 199X

Dear Sir,

I am writing to introduce myself and enquire whether you might
have any vacancies for receptionists at any of your hotels.

I am 25 years old and currently work as a receptionist at the
Beaumont Hotel in central London. I am fully experienced in
handling reservations, switchboard work, front office reception
duties and also accounts office work.

I am particularly interested in finding work in a tourist resort
and feel sure that I could contribute to the smooth running of
one of your hotels. I do know that your hotels receive a lot of
visitors from the UK, but I also speak a little Spanish and
German too.

I enclose my curriculum vitae which gives more details of my
qualifications and experience. If you have a job for which I
might be suitable I would be very interested to hear from you.

Yours faithfully,

Jane Jones.

Enclosed: CV.

Fig 4(b). A letter to a possible employer enquiring
about suitable vacancies.

Andrew Smith,
Recruitment Manager,
Platers Restaurants,
1 The High Street,
Anytown.
Sussex BN1 1AA

Michael Mitchell,
30 The Road,
Anytown,
Sussex BN1 1AA
Tel: 0123 999999
1 March 199X

Dear Mr. Smith,

I would like to apply for a place on your management training scheme as advertised in the Caterer and Hotelkeeper Careers Guide 199X.

I am 22 years old and at the moment I am studying for a BSc (Hons) degree in Hotel and Catering Management at the Anytown Metropolitan University, from which I expect to graduate this year.

As part of this course of study I have already spent 12 months working for a large contract catering company, which included three months working in Holland.

In addition to this I work during the evenings and weekends in a local fast food restaurant as a relief assistant manager. This has provided me with experience in many aspects of the retail catering business, including customer service, personnel and accounting.

I am very keen to make a career in the catering industry and am particularly interested in joining Platers Restaurants as I know they have a reputation for their high standard of training, and promotion of staff according to performance and merit.

I enclose my curriculum vitae which gives some more details about myself. If you feel I would be suitable for a place on your training scheme then I would be very pleased to attend for an interview.

Yours sincerely,

Michael Mitchell.

Enclosed: CV.

Fig 4(c). A letter to a company applying for a job which they have advertised.

CURRICULUM VITAE

Name/Nom/Name/Apellidos/Nome:

Address/Adresse/Anschrift/Dirección/Indirizzo:

Tel:

Date of birth/Date de naissance/Geburtsdatum/Fecha de nacimiento/Data di nascita:

Nationality/Nationalité/Staatsangehörigkeit/Nacionalidad/ Cittadinanza:

Education/Etudes/Ausbildungagang/Estudios/Studi:

Work experience/Expérience professionelle/ Berufserfahrung/Experiencia profesional/Esperienza professionale:

Fig. 5. Preparing an international-style CV, with the headings in English, French, German, Spanish and Italian.

Reference/Référence/Referenz/Referencia/Referenza (Attestato)

1.	2.

Interests outside work/Activités extra-professionelles/
Ausserberufliche/Actividades extra-profesionales/
Attività o attitudini extraprofessionali:

Other Information/Information supplémentaire/Zusätzlich
information/Información adicional/Informazioni supplementare:

Date/Date/Datum/Fecha/Date:

Fig. 5. Continued.

Fig. 6. Sample job advertisements.

HOTEL RECEPTIONIST
ASSISTANT HOUSEKEEPER
BARMAN/BARMAID
CHEF DE RANG
WAITER/WAITRESS
CONFERENCE AND LUGGAGE PORTER
BANQUETING STAFF

As a direct result of a number of recent internal promotions, and the increases in our business as the economy continues to improve, we are planning to recruit new people to join us.

The Richmond Hill Hotel, located halfway between Heathrow and Central London, is owned and operated by Securicor PLC, and is a leading member of the Best Western Consortium (UK). We provide 125 Quality Rooms and Suites supporting extensive banqueting and conference facilities at 3 Star standard.

If you feel that any of these vacancies will provide you with a welcome opportunity to change your job and advance your career we would like to hear from you. *Please apply in writing enclosing details of your career to date to:*

**BEST
WESTERN
HOTELS**

**Mr. James McMorrough,
General Manager,
Richmond Hill Hotel,
Richmond Hill,
Richmond upon Thames
TW10 6RW.
Tel: 081-940 2247**

Fig. 6. Sample job advertisements continued.

Fig. 6. Sample job advertisements continued.

HELP US GET THE SHOW ON THE ROAD.

Just as a Stage Manager or Director may be looking for style and panache at auditions, so too are we – for the recently restructured restaurant team at the Regents Park Marriott Hotel, a prestigious four star hotel with extensive facilities and a reputation for exceptional customer care.

We are looking for lively, out-going people who will really provide service with a smile and – after full training – a high degree of professionalism. In particular we seek:

RESTAURANT MANAGER – with around two years' sound relevant experience and a commitment to exceptional standards.

TEAM SUPERVISORS – with 18 months or more experience in a quality restaurant and proven supervisory ability.

WAITING STAFF – experience not essential provided you are quick to learn and have enthusiasm, energy and a lively extrovert personality. Flexibility is also needed as you will not only act as host and serve meals at tables, you will serve behind the bar, operate room service, and cashier.

We offer attractive rates of pay for a 39 hour week worked on a flexible rota; and our on-going training programmes ensure you have excellent prospects.

If you'd like to help us get the show on the road, please contact Andrew Lee, Personnel & Training Manager, the Regents Park Marriott, 128 King Henry's Road, London NW3 3ST, telephone 071-722 7711.

Marriott.
HOTELS · RESORTS · SUITES

Fig. 6. Sample job advertisements continued.

FORTE
RESTAURANTS

APPLICATION FOR A SUPERVISORY, MANAGERIAL OR ADMINISTRATIVE APPOINTMENT

Forte Plc is committed to a policy of treating all its employees and job applicants equally. To this end it undertakes to ensure that no actual or potential employee receives less favourable treatment or consideration on the grounds of race, colour, religion, nationality, ethnic origin, sex or marital status.

This form will be photocopied, please complete in block capitals in your own handwriting.

Position applied for:	How did this position come to your notice?
Salary expectation:	

Photograph is required
for all applicants

PERSONAL

Surname: Mr/Mrs/Miss/Ms	Address:
Forenames:	
	Postcode:
Previous Surname or Previous Names (including changes by deed poll):	Home Telephone No: STD ( ) Business Telephone No: STD ( )
Date of Birth: Age:	Name, Address & Telephone No. of Emergency Contact:
Place of Birth (Town & Country):	What is your Ethnic Origin? 3. European ☐ 1. Afro-Carribean ☐ 4. Oriental ☐ 2. Asian ☐ 5. Other ☐
Marital Status: Single/Married/Divorced/Separated/Widowed Number of Children: Ages of Children:	Have you a valid driving licence? Do you have any points on licence?
Are you willing to move? YES/NO If Yes, please specify any restrictions	Are you a car owner?
Have you ever been convicted of a crime or an offence? If Yes, give details:	

MEDICAL

Answers given to the following questions should be true to the best of your knowledge. If answering Yes please give details using a separate sheet if necessary.

What is your general state of health? Good ☐ Average ☐ Poor ☐

Have you, within the past three years, attended an out-patients clinic or had a course of treatment (Tablets, Injections or Physiotherapy) lasting one month or more? YES/NO

Are you now receiving any such treatment? YES/NO

Do you take regular medication YES/NO

Do you suffer from or have you ever suffered with: Ear, eye, nose or throat infection? YES/NO

Fits, epilepsy or blackouts? YES/NO   Diabetes? YES/NO   Depressive illness or nervous troubles? YES/NO

Skin disease or dermatitis? YES/NO   Allergies (to any drug or to handling any substance)? YES/NO

Have you travelled abroad or lived abroad within the past 30 days? If Yes, please state Country.

Are you on the Register of Disabled Persons? YES/NO   Give registration number

Fig. 7. Sample job application forms.

EMPLOYMENT RECORD

References will be taken up with your previous employers if you are offered a position with the Company but not with your present employer without your permission. Details must be given of ALL positions held in the last five years starting with your present or most recent position. Include any previous experience with Forte Plc. All periods of unemployment must also be shown, details must include the Benefit Office with which you were registered. Please continue on another sheet if necessary.

DATES		EMPLOYER'S NAME AND ADDRESS	POSITION HELD, YOUR MAIN DUTIES	PLEASE STATE PRESENT SALARY	FULL REASON FOR LEAVING	TO WHOM ENQUIRY SHOULD BE ADDRESSED FOR A REFERENCE NAME, ADDRESS AND TELEPHONE NUMBER
FROM MONTH YEAR	TO MONTH YEAR					
						Tel: ( )
						Tel: ( )
						Tel: ( )
						Tel: ( )
						Tel: ( )

Fig. 7. Sample job application forms continued.

Date available or Notice Period required by present employer:	Do you have any holiday commitments?

Give details of any relatives employed by Welcome Break or its associates:

Name   Relationship   Unit   Position

EDUCATION

Dates	Schools attended (from age 11 onwards):	Examinations passed/to be taken, give subjects and grades:

(Activities and responsibilities inside and outside school (societies, teams, offices held):

Dates	College/University attended, Course and Main Subjects:	Diplomas, Degrees, Distinctions, etc., gained or expected:

(Activities and responsibilities inside and outside College/University (societies, teams, offices held):

Special Qualifications, Membership of Professional Bodies

Languages, spoken or written (Please state degree of fluency)

LEISURE INTERESTS/VOLUNTARY WORK

Please give details of hobbies, sports, membership of clubs and societies, etc.

Fig. 7. Sample job application forms continued.

OTHER INFORMATION

Write down an example of when you worked the hardest and felt the greatest sense of achievement.

What have been the most important events or people in your own development and why?

REFERENCES

Referees   It is a condition of Employment that all applicants provide references covering their previous five years of continuous employment. Where any applicant has either been self-employed or has not been continuously employed over the previous five years then for those periods not covered by employment, references from the Department of Employment will suffice.

Applicants without any employment in the previous five years should provide the names, addresses and telephone numbers of three professional personal referees who we can contact for a reference (School Head, College Principal, etc.)

1.

2.

3.

I certify by signature that the information given in this form is true in every respect. I also give permission to Forte Welcome Break to contact the employment, professional and other referees listed in this application. I note that it is a condition that employment will be subject to the receipt of satisfactory references.

In certain jobs it is necessary for the company to obtain a security ID pass. If this requirement applies to your application, any offer of employment is also conditional upon our being able to obtain a security ID pass. To obtain a pass on Airports, proof of identity and copies of references will need to be supplied under a confidentiality agreement to the Airport Authority in the common interest of security. By signing below you indicate your understanding to our passing on the aforementioned details to the relevant authority.

Signature... Date...

Fig. 7. Sample job application forms continued.

HILTON

APPLICATION

FOR

EMPLOYMENT

NAME:

POSITION APPLIED FOR:

Hilton U.K. (a part of the Ladbroke Group PLC) is an Equal Opportunities Employer. We welcome applications from all members of the community regardless of sex, age, marital status, race, ethnic origin or disability.

Should you have any difficulty in completing this application form please inform me so that I may assist you.

Thank you for your interest in Hilton U.K.

Personnel Manager

Please return this form to:

Fig. 7. Sample job application forms continued.

EQUAL OPPORTUNITIES WITHIN HILTON U.K.

Hilton U.K. is committed to Equal Opportunities for all. This means that everyone that we employ or who works for us is treated equally, whatever their gender, marital status, race, colour, age or ethnic origins.

We need to ensure that our policy is working in practice and, to help us, we ask you to provide the following information about yourself. Should you be successful in your application for employment, this information will be transferred onto a confidential file that holds records of all the people working for Hilton U.K. throughout the country.

The information provided will be separated from this application form and will be used solely for monitoring purposes. It does not form part of the selection process.

Position applied for:

_____

Date of birth: / /

Place of birth:

Sex: Male/Female

Nationality:

MARITAL STATUS

Divorced ☐   Married ☐

Single ☐   Widowed ☐

Other ☐

I am ☐ am not ☐ a disabled person.

Nature of disability:_____

Registration No:_____

ETHNIC ORIGIN

ASIAN

Bangladeshi ☐   Chinese ☐

Indian ☐   Pakistani ☐

U.K. ☐   Other ☐

Please specify: _____

BLACK

African ☐   Caribbean ☐

U.K. ☐   Other ☐

Please specify: _____

WHITE

Irish ☐   U.K. ☐

European ☐   Other ☐

Please Specify: _____

NONE OF THE ABOVE

Please Specify: _____

SIGNATURE: _____   **DATE:** _____

Fig. 7. Sample job application forms continued.

APPLICATION FOR EMPLOYMENT

Private and confidential
(Please can you complete this form using Block Capitals)

Position applied for:

Where did you hear of this vacancy:

PERSONAL DETAILS

Surname: Mr/Miss/Mrs/Ms
(Please include any previous names if applicable)

Forenames:

Permanent Address:

Correspondence Address:
(If different)

Daytime Telephone Number:

Date of Birth:

Evening Telephone Number:

HISTORY OF EDUCATION

From Month/Year	To Month/Year	School/College/University Name and Address	Subjects taken	Qualifications Gained

---

CURRENT EMPLOYMENT

Name of Company:

Address:

Telephone:

Contact Name:

Current Position:

Date of Commencement:

Period of Notice:

Fig. 7. Sample job application forms continued.

PREVIOUS EMPLOYMENT

From (Exact Dates)	To (Exact Dates)	Name/Address/Tel. of Employer	Position held Outline of duties & Final salary	Reason for Leaving

ADDITIONAL INFORMATION

Have you ever had any serious illness, injury or operation?　　　　YES/NO
If yes, please give dates and details:

Have you ever been found guilty of any criminal, civil or military offence?　　　YES/NO
If yes, please give dates and details:

Are you prepared to work in any Hilton Hotel within the UK?　　　YES/NO
If no, please state preferred location:

OTHER INFORMATION

Please give any further information you feel will support your application: (Include why you wish to work for Hilton, main responsibilities and achievements in your last job, leisure interests and activities)

I certify that the information given by me on this form is correct and that if I have given false information or deliberately omitted any relevant facts, this could lead to my dismissal.

I agree that you may approach any of my previous employers for a reference, and I understand that you will not approach my present employer until an offer of employment is made.

Signature of Applicant:　　　　　　　　　　　　　Date:

Fig. 7. Sample job application forms continued.

5
The Hotel and Catering Industry in the United Kingdom

HOTELS AND CATERING IN THE UK

The hospitality industry in the UK is one of the largest in Europe. It employs 2.4 million people and is expected to grow by over 7% by the turn of the century.

Many of the companies in the industry are currently planning expansion, despite the recession, and some of them are expanding into other countries, particularly France, Germany, Spain and Ireland. In some cases there is a shortage of skilled and qualified people for certain jobs, and the leading hospitality companies compete vigorously with each other to recruit the best people.

The main parts of the business are Hotels and Catering.

Hotels
The hotel business in the UK is basically run by three types of organisation — large groups, small groups and privately owned hotels.

Large groups
The large groups, like Forte and Hilton, own many hotels, and they are often divided into several brands: for example, Forte Grand (luxury hotels) and Forte Travelodge (inexpensive motel-type accommodation).

Small groups
Small groups, like Scottish Highland Hotels, own a smaller number of hotels, often specialising in just one area.

Privately owned hotels
Privately owned hotels are owned and run by just one person, or by a small company. They usually own only one property, and often the proprietors work in the business themselves.

Note

In many cases the groups offer the best training; almost all of them recruit the inexperienced for regular staff and management training schemes. They also offer promotion to some of the biggest and best hotels in the country, and worldwide. However, privately owned hotels should not be ignored. There is often less competition for the jobs they have, especially for those who are not school leavers, and it is quite possible to start at a small hotel and then, once experienced, apply to work with one of the groups.

Catering

The catering industry in the UK is much less easy to understand than the hotel industry. There have been major changes in the industry in the last few years — such the catering in many offices and factories now being operated by contract catering companies, rather than by the office or factory owners.

The easiest division to make is between leisure catering, and institutional and contract catering. Institutional and contract catering provides catering to fill a need, such as when people are at school or at work. Leisure catering covers pubs and restaurants, in other words somewhere people go for entertainment and enjoyment. Many jobs in either area are similar, but it is important to remember the subtle difference.

Leisure catering

On the leisure side there are two types of company:

- **Large groups**: Large companies operating catering operations all over the country: for example, McDonalds, Welcome Break service stations or Beefeater Restaurants. In some cases these are franchises — individually owned outlets operating under a well-known name — rather than wholly company owned. This applies to KFC. In many cases if the name is known worldwide the UK operation is quite separate from that in other countries. This applies to Pizza Hut.

- **Privately owned caterers**: Privately owned catering businesses are usually owned and operated by just one person, who often works in the business themselves. This includes many restaurants, many pubs, and your local fish and chip shop.

There are very few small groups in the leisure catering business.

Contract and institutional catering
Most contract and institutional catering locations are run as part of large or very large companies. For example, Catering and Allied operates 90 staff restaurants in the London area alone. Russell and Brand operate 200 catering contracts and plan to increase this to almost 300 over the next year.

Whether in leisure or contract and institutional catering, most of the large catering companies have very well-organised training programmes and offer good promotion prospects. They have made great efforts over recent years to present catering as a good career choice.

For many smaller caterers, training is a less important consideration and promotion prospects are much fewer. The new NVQ qualification should particularly help people who choose to work in this area.

Tips
When choosing an employer in the hospitality industry consider:

● What type of company is it?

● What sort of training facilities do they have?

● What opportunities for promotion are there?

● What types of work are available (see Chapter 3)?

UNIVERSITIES AND COLLEGES OFFERING DEGREE COURSES

(Universities offering HCIMA qualifications are also shown. For COLLEGES offering HCIMA qualifications see next section.)

Aberdeen: Robert Gordon University, Aberdeen AB9 2PG. Tel: (01224) 633611. BA (Hons) Hospitality Management.

Birmingham College of Food, Tourism & Creative Studies (with De Montford University). BA (Hons) Hotel Business Management.

Birmingham (University of Central England), Birmingham B42 2SU. Tel: (0121) 235 2157. BA (Hons) Hospitality Management.

Blackpool and the Fylde College. BA (Hons) Hospitality Management, BA Hotel, Catering and Institutional Management.

Bournemouth University, Talbot Campus, Bournemouth BH12 5BB. Tel: (01202) 524111. BA (Hons) Hospitality Management, BSc (Hons) Food and Catering Management.

Brighton, University of, 49 Darley Road, Eastbourne BN20 7UR. Tel: (01273) 643614. BA (Hons) International Hospitality Management.

Buckingham, University of. BSc (Hons) Business Studies (International Hotel Management). (An independent university).

Cardiff Institute of HE. BA Hotel Management.

Cheltenham & Gloucester College of HE. BA (Hons) Hotel Management, Catering Management, Tourism Management, Leisure Management.

Clarendon College, Nottingham. BA (Hons) Hotel and Catering.

Colchester Institute. BA Business Studies (Catering Management).

College of Cardiff, University of Wales, 65 Park Place, Cardiff CF1 3AS. Tel: (01222) 874846. BSc (Hons) Hotel and Institutional Management.

Derby Tertiary College. BSc (Hons) Hospitality Management.

Edinburgh: Napier University, 10 Colinton Road, Edinburgh EH10 5DT. Tel: (0131) 455 2571. BA (Hons) Hospitality Management.

Edinburgh: Queen Margaret College. BA Hospitality Enterprise with Tourism.

Glasgow: Queen's College. BA (Hons) Hospitality Management.

Glasgow: University of Strathclyde, Cathedral Street, Glasgow G4 0LG. Tel: (0141) 552 4400. BA (Hons) Hotel and Catering Management.

Guildford: University of Surrey, Stag Hill, Guildford GU2 5XH. Tel: (01483) 300800. BSc (Hons) Hotel and Catering Management, BSc Hotel Management.

Highbury College, Portsmouth. BA (Hons) Hotel and Catering Management.

Huddersfield, The University of, Huddersfield HD1 3DH. Tel: (01484) 422288. BA (Hons) Hotel and Catering Business.

Leeds Metropolitan University, Calverley Street, Leeds LS1 3HE. Tel: (0113) 2832600. BA (Hons) Hospitality Business Management, BSc (Hons) Hospitality Management and Related Services.

London: Middlesex University, Hendon NW4 4BT. Tel: (0181) 362 5000. BSc (Hons) Hotel and Restaurant Management.

London: South Bank University, 103 Borough Road, London SE1 0AA. Tel: (0171) 928 8989. BA (Hons) Hotel Management.

London: Thames Valley University, St Mary's Road, London W5 5RF. Tel: (0181) 579 5000. BA (Hons) Hospitality Management, HCIMA Cert.

London: University of North London, Holloway Road, London N7 8DB. Tel: (0171) 607 2789. BA (Hons) International Hotel and Catering Management.

Manchester Metropolitan University, Manchester M14 6HR. Tel:

(0161) 247 2722. BSc (Hons) Hotel and Catering Management, BA (Hons) International Hotel Management, HCIMA Dip.

Norwich City College of Further and Higher Education. BA (Hons) Hospitality Management.

Nottingham: Trent University, Nottingham NG1 4BU. Tel: (0115) 9486414. BA (Hons) International Hospitality Management, BA (Hons) Hotel and Catering Management.

Oxford: Brookes University, Headington, Oxford OX3 0BP. Tel: (01865) 819800. BSc/BA (Hons) Catering Management/Tourism, BSc (Hons) Hotel and Catering Management, HCIMA Dip.

Paisley: Reid Kerr College. BSc Quality Management & Technology for Hospitality.

Plymouth, University of (with South Devon and Plymouth College of HE), Newton Abbot TQ12 6NQ. Tel: (01626) 325643. BSc (Hons) Hospitality Management.

Portsmouth, University of, Milton, Southsea PO4 8JF. Tel: (01705) 827681. BA (Hons) Hotel and Catering Management.

Preston: University of Central Lancashire, Preston PR1 2HE. Tel: (01772) 893770. BA (Hons) Hospitality Management.

Salford: University College, Salford M6 6PU. Tel: (0161) 736 6541. BA (Hons) Hospitality Management, HCIMA Cert.

Sheffield: Hallam University, Pond Street, Sheffield S1 1WB. Tel: (0114) 2533325. BSc (Hons) Hotel and Catering Management, BSc (Hons) Hotel and Tourism Management, HCIMA Dip.

Torquay: South Devon College. BSc Hospitality Management.

Ulster, University of, Newtownabbey BT38 0QB. Tel: (01232) 365131. BA (Hons) Hospitality Management, BA (Hons) Hotel and Tourism Management.

Wolverhampton University, Compton Park, Wolverhampton WV3 9DX. Tel: (01902) 323629. BA (Hons) Hotel Management/Tourism Management, Licensed Retail Management/International Hospitality Management.

Addresses and telephone numbers for colleges are given in the next section.

COLLEGES OFFERING NVQ, GNVQ, BTEC & HCIMA QUALIFICATIONS

N — NVQs	S — SVQs
G — GNVQs	GS — GSVQs
B — BTEC	SV — SCOTVEC
H — HCIMA	

A

Aberdare College, Cymdare Road, Aberdare CF44 8ST. Tel: (01685) 873405. N, G, B.

Aberdeen College, Gallowgate, Aberdeen AB9 1DN. Tel: (01224) 612188. S, SV.

Abingdon College, Northcourt Road, Abingdon OX14 1NN. Tel: (01235) 555585. N.

Accrington and Rossendale College, Blackburn Road, Accrington BB5 0AQ. Tel: (01254) 393521. N, B.

Angus College, Keptie Road, Arbroath DD11 3EA. Tel: (01241) 72056. SV.

Antrim Technical College, Antrim BT41 4AL; Tel: (018494) 63916. N, G.

Armagh College of FE, Lonsdale Street, Armagh BT6 4TF. Tel: (01861) 522205.

Aylesbury College, Oxford Road, Aylesbury HP21 8PD. Tel: (01296) 434111. N, G, B, H.

Ayr College, Dam Park, Ayr KA8 0EU. Tel: (01292) 265184. S, GS, SV.

B

Ballymena College, Farm Lodge Avenue, Ballymena BT43 7DJ. Tel: (01266) 652871. N, G.

Banbridge College of FE, Banbridge BT32 4AX. Tel: (018206) 62289. N.

Banff and Buchan College, Fraserburgh AB43 5GA. Tel: (01346) 515777. S, SV.

Bath College, Avon Street, Bath BA1 1UP. Tel: (01225) 312191. N, G, B.

Barking College, Dagenham Road, Romford RM7 0XU. Tel: (01708) 766841. N.

Barnet College, Wood Street, London EN5 4PG. Tel: (0181) 440 6321. N.

Barnfield College, New Bedford Road, Luton LU3 9BF. Tel: (01582) 507531. N, G, H.

Barnsley College, Church Street, Barnsley S70 2AX. Tel: (01226) 730191. N, G, B.

Barry College, Colcott Road, Barry, S.Glam CF6 8YJ. Tel: (01446) 743519. N, G.

Basingstoke College of Technology, Worthing Road, Basingstoke RG21 1TN. Tel: (01256) 54141. N, G, B, H.

Bedford College of HE, Cauldwell Street, Bedford MK42 9AH. Tel: (01234) 345151. N, G, B.

Belfast Institute of Further and Higher Education, Belfast BT2 7GX. Tel: (01232) 245891. N, G, B, H.

Beverley College, Gallows Lane, Beverley HU17 7DT. Tel: (01482) 868362. N, G.

Bilston Community College, Westfield Road, Bilston, Wolverhampton WV14 6ER. Tel: (01902) 323629. N, G.

Birmingham College of Food, Tourism & Creative Studies, Summer Row, Birmingham B3 1JB. Tel: (0121) 604 1000. N, G, B.

Blackburn College, Feilden Street, Blackburn BB1 1LH. Tel: (01254) 55144. N, G, B.

Blackpool and the Fylde College, Ashfield Road, Bispham, Blackpool FY2 0HB. Tel: (01253) 352352. N, G, B, H.

Bolton College, Manchester Road, Bolton BL2 1ER. Tel: (01204) 31411. N, G, H.

Borders College, Commercial Road, Hawick TD9 7AW. Tel: (01450) 74191. GS, SV.

Boston College of FE, Rowley Road, Boston PE21 6JF. Tel: (01205) 365701. N, G, B.

Bournemouth and Poole College of FE, The Lansdowne, Bournemouth BH1 3JJ. Tel: (01202) 747600. N, G, H.

Bournville College of FE, Bristol Road South, Birmingham B31 2AJ. Tel: (0121) 411 1414. N.

Bracknell College, Church Road, Bracknell RG12 1DJ. Tel: (01344) 420411. N, G.

Bradford & Ilkley Community College, Great Horton Road, Bradford BD7 1AY. Tel: (01274) 753004. N, G, B.

Braintree College, Church Lane, Braintree CM7 5SN. Tel: (01376) 321711. N.

Bridgend College, Cowbridge Road, Bridgend, W.Glam CF31 3DF. Tel: (01656) 766588. N, B.

Brighton College of Technology, Pelham Street, Brighton BN1 4FA. Tel: (01273) 667788. N, G, B, H.

Brockenhurst College, Lyndhurst Road, Brockenhurst, Hants SO42 7ZE. Tel: (01590) 23565. N, B.

Brooklands College, Heath Road, Weybridge KT13 8TT. Tel: (01932) 853300. N, G.

Brunel College of Arts and Technology, Ashley Down Road, Bristol BS7 9BU. Tel: (0117) 9241241. N, G, B, H.

Burton Upon Trent Technical College, Lichfield Street, Burton Upon Trent DE14 3RL. Tel: (01283) 45401. N, G, H.

Bury College, Albert Road, Whitfield, Bury M25 6NH. Tel: (0161) 763 2501. N, G.

C

Calderdale College, Francis Street, Halifax HX1 3UZ. Tel: (01422) 358221. N, G.

Cambridge Regional College, Newmarket Road, Cambridge CB5 8EG. Tel: (01223) 324455. N, G, B.

Cambuslang College, East Kilbride G74 4JZ. Tel: (013552) 43018. GS, SV.

Cannock Chase Technical College, The Green, Cannock WS11 1UE. Tel: (01543) 462200. N, G.

Canterbury College, New Dover Road, Canterbury CT1 3AJ. Tel: (01227) 766081. N, G.

Cardiff Institute of HE, Colchester Road, Cardiff CF3 7XR. Tel: (01222) 551111. N, G, B.

Carlisle College, Victoria Place, Carlisle CA1 1HS. Tel: (01228) 24464. N, G.

Carmarthenshire College of Technology and Art, Pibwrlwyd Campus, Carmarthen SA31 2NH. N, G, B.

Carshalton College, Nightingale Road, Carshalton SM5 2EJ. Tel: (0181) 770 6800. N, G, B.

Castlereagh College of FE, Belfast BT6 9JD. Tel: (01232) 797144. N, G, B.

Causeway Institute, 2 Coleraine Road, Ballymoney BT53 6BP. Tel: (012656) 62258. N.

Chelmsford College of FE, Princes Road, Chelmsford CM2 9DX. Tel: (01245) 265611. N, G, B, H.

Cheltenham and Gloucester College of HE, Swindon Road, Cheltenham GL50 4AZ. Tel: (01242) 532824. B.

Chesterfield College, Infirmary Road, Chesterfield S41 7NG. Tel: (01246) 231212. N.

Chichester College of Arts, Science and Technology, Westgate Fields, Chichester PO19 1SB. Tel: (01243) 786321. N, G, B.

Chippenham College, Cocklebury Road, Chippenham SN15 3QD. Tel: (01249) 444501. N, G.

City of Liverpool College, Colquitt Centre, Liverpool L1 4DB. Tel: (0151) 709 0541. N, B.

City College Norwich, Ipswich Road, Norwich NR2 2LJ. Tel: (01603) 660011. N, G, B, H.

Clackmannan College of FE, Branshill Road, Alloa FK10 3BT. Tel: (01259) 215121. GS, SV.

Clarendon College, Pelham Avenue, Nottingham NG5 1AL. Tel: (0115) 9691418. N, G, B, H.

Clydebank College, Kilbowie Road, Clydebank G81 2AA. Tel: (0141) 952 7771. S, GS, SV.

Coalville Technical College, Bridge Road, Coalville LE6 2QR. Tel: (01530) 836136. N.

Colchester Institute, Sheepen Road, Colchester CO3 3LL. Tel: (01206) 718000. N, G, B.

Coleg Ceredigion, Rhdyfelin, Aberystwyth SY23 3PB. Tel: (01970) 612487. N.

Coleg Ceredigion, Park Place, Cardigan SA43 1AB. Tel: (01239) 612032. N.

Coleg Meirion-Dwyfor, Dolgellau, Gwynedd LL40 2SW. Tel: (01341) 422827. N, G.

Coleg Pencraig, Ynys Mon, Llangefni, Gwynedd LL77 7HY. Tel: (01248) 750101. N, G.

Coleg Powys Brecon, Penlan, Brecon LD3 9SR. Tel: (01874) 625252. N, G.

Coleg Powys Montgomery, Llanidoes Road, Newtown SY16 4HY. Tel: (01686) 622722. N, G, B.

College of North West London, Priory Park Road, Kilburn NW6 7UJ. Tel: (0171) 328 8241. N.

Cumbernauld College, Cumbernauld G67 1HU. Tel: (01236) 731811. GS, SV.

Cornwall College, Redruth TR15 3RD. Tel: (01209) 712911. N, G, B, H.

Craven College, High Street, Skipton BD23 1JY. Tel: (01756) 791411. N, G, B.

Crawley College, College Road, Crawley RH10 1NR. Tel: (01293) 612686. N, G, H.

Cricklade College, Charlton Road, Andover SP10 1EJ. Tel: (01264) 363311. N, B.

Croydon College, Fairfield, Croydon CR9 1DX. Tel: (0181) 686 5700. N, G, B, H.

D

Darlington College of Technology, Cleveland Avenue, Darlington DL3 7BB. Tel: (01325) 467651. N, G.

Deeside College of FE, Kelsterton Road, Connah's Quay, CH5 4BB. Tel: (01244) 831531. N, G.

Derby College, London Road, Wilmorton, Derby DE24 8UG. Tel: (01332) 757570. N, G, B.

Derwentside College, Park Road, Consett DH8 5EE. Tel: (01207) 502906. N.

Dewsbury College, Halifax Road, Dewsbury WF13 2AS. Tel: (01924) 465916. N, G.

Doncaster College, Waterdale, Doncaster DN1 3EX. Tel: (01302) 322122. N, G.

Down College of FE, Downpatrick BT30 6ND. Tel: (01396) 615816. N, G, B.

Dumfries and Galloway College of Technology, Dumfries DG1 3QZ. Tel: (01387) 61261. S, GS.

Duncan of Jordanstone College, Perth Road, Dundee DD1 4HT. Tel: (01382) 23261. SV.

Dundee College, Old Glamis Road, Dundee DD3 8LE. Tel: (01382) 819021. S, GS, SV.

E

Eastbourne College of Arts and Technology, Kings Drive, Eastbourne BN21 2UN. Tel: (01323) 644711. N, G, B.

East Birmingham College, Garretts Green Lane, Sheldon, Birmingham B33 0TS. Tel: (0121) 743 4471. N, G.

East Devon College, Bolham Road, Tiverton EX16 6SH. Tel: (01884) 254247. N, G, B.

East Surrey College, College Crescent, Redhill RH1 2FA. Tel: (01737) 772611. N, G.

East Tyrone College of FE, Circular Road, Dungannon BT71 6BQ. Tel: (018687) 22323. N, G, B.

East Warwickshire College, Lower Hilmorton Road, Rugby CV21 3QS. Tel: (01788) 541666. N, G.

East Yorkshire College, St Mary's Walk, Bridlington YO16 5JW. Tel: (01262) 672676. N, G, B.

Eastleigh College, Chestnut Avenue, Eastleigh SO5 5HT. Tel: (01703) 326326. N, G.

Elmwood College of FE, Carslogie Road, Cupar, Fife KY15 4JB. Tel: (01334) 52781. S, SV.

Exeter College, Hele Road, Exeter EX4 4JS. Tel: (01392) 384000. N, G, B, H.

F

Falkirk College of Technology, Falkirk FK2 9AD. Tel: (01324) 24981. GS, SV.

Fareham College, Bishopsfield Road, Fareham PO14 1NH. Tel: (01329) 221110. N, G.

Farnborough College of Technology, Boundary Road, Farnborough GU14 6SB. Tel: (01252) 515511. N, G, B.

Fermanagh College, Dublin Road, Enniskillen BT74 6AE. Tel: (01365) 322431. N, G, B.

Fife College of Further and Higher Education, Kirkcaldy KY1 1EX. Tel: (01592) 268591. S, GS, SV.

Furness College, Howard Street, Barrow in Furness LA14 1NB. Tel: (01229) 825017. N, G.

G

Glasgow College of Food Technology, Glasgow G1 2TG. Tel: (0141) 552 3751. S, GS, SV, HCIMA.

Glenrothes College, Stenton Road, Glenrothes KY6 2RA. Tel: (01592) 772233. GS, SV.

Gloucestershire College of Arts & Technology, 73 The Park, Cheltenham GL50 2RR. Tel: (01242) 532073. N, G.

Grantham College, Stonebridge Road, Grantham NG31 9AP. Tel: (01476) 63141. N, G.

Great Yarmouth College, Southtown, Great Yarmouth NR31 0ED. Tel: (01493) 655261. N, G.

Grimsby College, Nuns' Corner, Grimsby DN34 5BQ. Tel: (01472) 29943. N, B.

Guildford College of Further and Higher Education, Stoke Park, Guildford GU1 1EZ. Tel: (01483) 31251. N, G, B.

Guernsey College of FE, Route des Coutanchez, St Peter Port, Guernsey GY1 2TT. Tel: (01481) 727121. N, G.

Gwent Tertiary College, Ebbw Vale NP3 6LE. Tel: (01495) 302083. N.

Gwent Tertiary College, Crosskeys NP1 7ZA. Tel: (01495) 271295. N, B.

Gwent Tertiary College, Newport NP9 9HG. Tel: (01633) 274861. N, B.

Gwent Tertiary College, Tympath Road, Pontypool NP4 6AQ. Tel: (01495) 762242. N, G, B.

H

Halesowen College, Whittingham Road, Halesowen B63 3NA. Tel: (0121) 550 1451. N, B.

Halton College of FE, Kingsway, Widnes WA8 7QQ. Tel: (0151) 423 1391. N, G.

Handsworth College, Soho Road, Handsworth, Birmingham B21 9DP. Tel: (0121) 743 4471. N.

Harlow College, College Square, The High, Harlow CM20 1LT. Tel: (01279) 441288. N, G.

Harrogate College, Hornbeam Park, Hookstone Road, Harrogate HG2 8QT. Tel: (01423) 879466. N, G.

Hastings College of Arts and Technology, Archery Road, St Leonards on Sea TN38 0HX. Tel: (01424) 423847. N, B.

Havering College of Further and Higher Education, Tring Gardens, Harold Hill, Romford RM3 9ES. Tel: (01708) 381460. N, B.

Hendon College, Grahame Park Way, London NW9 5RA. Tel: (0181) 200 8300. N, B.

Henley College Coventry, Henley Road, Bell Green, Coventry CV2 1ED. Tel: (01203) 611021. N, G.

Herefordshire College of Technology, Folly Lane, Hereford HR1 1LS. Tel: (01432) 352235. N, G, B, H.

Hertford Regional College, Scotts Road, Ware SG12 9JF. Tel: (01920) 465441. N, G.

High Peak College, Harpur Hill, Buxton SK17 9JZ. Tel: (01298) 71100. N, G, B, H.

Highbury College, Dovercourt Road, Cosham, Portsmouth PO6 2SA. Tel: (01705) 383131. N, G, B.

Highlands College, PO Box 1000, St Saviour, Jersey JE4 9QA. Tel: (01534) 608550. N, G, B, H.

Hinckley College of FE, London Road, Hinckley LE10 1XR. Tel: (01455) 251222. N.

Hopwood Hall Tertiary College, Rochdale OL12 6RY. Tel: (01706) 345346. N, B.

Huddersfield Technical College, New North Road, Huddersfield HD1 5NN. Tel: (01484) 536521. N, G, B.

Hugh Baird College, Church Road, Litherland, Liverpool L21 5HA. Tel: (0151) 934 4463.

Hull College, Queens Gardens, Hull HU1 3DG. Tel: (01482) 29943. N, G, B, H.

I

Inverness College, 3 Longman Road, Inverness IV1 1SA. Tel: (01463) 236681. S, GS, SV.

Isle of Man College, Homefield Road, Douglas, Isle of Man. Tel: (01624) 623113. N, B.

Isle of Wight College, Medina Way, Newport PO30 5TA. Tel: (01983) 526631. N, G, B.

J

James Watt College, Finnart Street, Greenock PA16 8HF. Tel: (01475) 24433. S, GS, SV.

Jewel and Esk Valley College, Dalkeith EH22 3AE. Tel: (0131) 663 1951. S, GS, SV.

John Wheatley College, 1346 Shettleston Road, Glasgow G32 9AT. Tel: (0141) 763 2384. S, SV.

K

Kendal College of FE, Milnthorpe Road, Kendal LA9 5AY. Tel: (01539) 724313. N, G, B, H.

Kilmarnock College, Irvine KA12 0LP. Tel: (01294) 311259. GS, SV.

Kirby College, Roman Road, Middlesbrough TS5 5PJ. Tel: (01642) 813706. N, G, B.

Kirkwall College of FE, Kirkwall, Orkney KW15 1QN. Tel: (01856) 872839. S, SV.

Knowsley Community College, Rupert Road, Huyton, Liverpool L36 9TD. Tel: (0151) 443 2600. N, B.

L

Lancaster and Morecambe College, Morecambe Road, Lancaster LA1 2TY. Tel: (01524) 843078. N, G, B.

Larne College of FE, Pond Street, Larne BT40 1SQ. Tel: (01574) 272268. N, G, B.

Leicester South Fields College, Aylestone Road, Leicester LE2 7LW. Tel: (0116) 2541818. N, G, B.

Lews Castle College, Stornoway, Lewis PA86 0XR. Tel: (01851) 703311. S, GS, SV.

Lewisham College, Breakspears Road, Lewisham Way, London SE4 1UT. Tel: (0181) 692 3353. N, G, B, H.

Limavady College of FE, Main Street, Limavady BT49 0EX. Tel: (015047) 62334. N.

Lisburn College, Castle Street, Lisburn BT27 4SU. Tel: (01846) 677225. N, G.

Llandrillo College, Llandudno Road, Rhos on Sea, Colwyn Bay LL28 4HZ. Tel: (01492) 546666. N, G, B, H.

Loughborough College, Radmoor, Loughborough LE11 3BT. Tel: (01509) 215831. N, G, B.

Lowestoft College, St Peter's Street, Lowestoft NR32 2NB. Tel: (01502) 583521. N, G.

Lurgan College of FE, Kitchen Hill, Lurgan BT66 6AZ. Tel: (01762) 326135.

M

Macclesfield College, Park Lane, Macclesfield SK11 8LF. Tel: (01625) 427744. N, B.

Magherafelt College of FE, 22 Moneymore Road, Magherafelt BT45 6AE. N.

Manchester College of Arts and Technology, Lower Hardman Street, Manchester M3 3ER. Tel: (0161) 953 5995. N, G.

Melton Mowbray College, Asfordby Road, Melton Mowbray LE13 0HJ. Tel: (01664) 67431. N, G.

Merthyr Tydfil College, Ynysfach, Merthyr Tydfil CF48 1AR. Tel: (01685) 723663. N.

Merton College, London Road, Morden SM4 5QX. Tel: (0181) 640 3001. N, G.

Mid Cheshire College of FE, Hartford Campus, Northwich CW8 1LJ. Tel: (01606) 75281. N, G, B.

Mid Kent College of Higher and Further Education, Tonbridge Road, Maidstone ME16 8AQ. Tel: (01622) 691555. N, G.

Milton Keynes College, Bletchley Centre, Sherwood Drive, Bletchley, Milton Keynes MK3 6DR. Tel: (01908) 668998. N, B, H.

Monkwearmouth College, Swan Street, Sunderland SR5 1EB. Tel: (0191) 516 2000. N, B.

Moray College, Moray Street, Elgin IV30 1NX. Tel: (01343) 554305. S, GS, SV.

Motherwell College, Dalzell Drive, Motherwell ML1 2DD. Tel: (01698) 259641. GS, SV, H.

N

Neath College, Dwr-y-Felin Road, Neath SA10 7RF. Tel: (01639) 634271. N, B.

Nelson and Colne College, Scotland Road, Nelson BB9 7YT. Tel: (01282) 603151. N, B.

New College Durham, Framwellgate Moor, Durham DH1 5ES. Tel: (0191) 386 2421. N, G.

Newbury College of FE, Oxford Road, Newbury RG13 1PQ. Tel: (01635) 37000. N, G.

Newcastle College, Sandyford Road, Newcastle Upon Tyne NE1 8QE. Tel: (0191) 227 4226. N, G, B, H.

Newcastle College of FE, 2 Donard Street, Newcastle, N Ireland BT33 0AP. Tel: (013967) 24613. N.

Newham Community College, Welfare Road, Stratford, London E15 4HT. Tel: (0181) 555 1422. N, B.

Newry College of FE, Patrick Street, Newry BT35 8DN. Tel: (01693) 61071. N, G, B.

Newtownabbey FE College, Portrush BT56 8JL. Tel: (01265) 823768. N, G, B.

Norfolk College, Tennyson Avenue, Kings Lynn PE30 2QW. Tel: (01553) 761144. N, B.

North Area College, Buckingham Road, Heath Moor, Stockport SK4 4RA. Tel: (0161) 442 7494. N, G.

North Derbyshire Tertiary College, Rectory Road, Clowne, Chesterfield S43 4BQ. Tel: (01246) 810332. N.

North Devon College, Sticklepath Hill, Barnstaple EX31 2BQ. Tel: (01271) 388018. N, G, B.

North Down and Ards College, Newtownards BT23 3ED. Tel: (01247) 812116. N.

North Down and Ards College, Bangor BT20 4TF. Tel: (01247) 271254. N, G, B.

North East Worcestershire College, Peakman Street, Redditch B98 8DW. Tel: (01527) 572867. N, G, B.

North Hertfordshire College, Broadway, Letchworth SG6 3PB. Tel: (01462) 683911. N, G, B, H.

North Lincolnshire College, Cathedral Street, Lincoln LN2 5HQ. Tel: (01522) 510530. N, G, B, H.

North Nottinghamshire College, Carlton Road, Worksop S81 7HP. Tel: (01909) 473561. N.

North Oxfordshire College and School of Art, Broughton Road, Banbury OX16 9QA. Tel: (01295) 252221. N.

North Tyneside College, Embleton Avenue, Wallsend NE28 9NJ. Tel: (0191) 262 4081. N, G, B.

North Warwickshire College, Hinckley Road, Nuneaton CV11 6BH. Tel: (01203) 349321. N, G, B.

North West Kent College of Technology, Miskin Road, Dartford DA1 1LU. Tel: (01322) 225471. N, G, B.

North West Institute, Strand Road, Londonderry BT48 7RY. Tel: (01504) 266711. N, G.

Northern Ireland Hotel and Catering College, Ballywillan Road, Portrush BT56 8JL. Tel: (01265) 823768. N, G, B.

Northampton College, Booth Lane, Northampton NN3 3RF. Tel: (01604) 734240. N, G.

Northbrook College of Design Technology, Littlehampton Road, Goring by Sea BN12 6NV. Tel: (01903) 830057. N, G.

Northumberland College of Arts and Technology, College Road, Ashington NE63 9RG. Tel: (01623) 27191. N, G, B.

North Lindsey College, Kingsway, Scunthorpe DN17 1AJ. Tel: (01724) 281111. N, G.

O

Oldham College, Rochdale Road, Oldham OL9 6AA. Tel: (0161) 624 5214. N, G, B.

Omagh College of FE, Omagh BT79 7AH. Tel: (01662) 245433. N, G.

Oxford College of FE, Oxpens Road, Oxford OX1 1SA. Tel: (01865) 245871. N, G, B.

P

Pembrokeshire College, Dew Street, Haverfordwest SA16 1SZ. Tel: (01437) 765247. N, G, B.

Perth College, Crieff Road, Perth PH1 2NX. Tel: (01738) 21171. S, GS, SV

Peterborough Regional College, Park Crescent, Peterborough PE1 4DZ. Tel: (01733) 67366. N, G.

Peterlee College, Peterlee SR8 1NU. Tel: (0191) 586 2225. N.

Portadown College of FE, 26 Lurgan Road, Portadown BT63 5BL. Tel: (01762) 337111. N, G, B.

Preston College, St Vincent Road, Fulwood, Preston PR2 4UR. Tel: (01772) 716511. N, G, B.

Plymouth College of FE, Kings Road, Devonport, Plymouth PL1 5QC. Tel: (01752) 385186. N, G, B, H.

Pontypridd College, Ynys Terrace, Rhydyfelin CF37 5RN. Tel: (01443) 486121. N.

Q

Queen Margaret College, Clerwood Terrace, Edinburgh EH4 2NZ. Tel: (0131) 317 3000. SV, HCIMA.

R

Reading College, Crescent Road, Reading RG1 5RQ. Tel: (01734) 583501. N, G, B.

Redbridge College of FE, Little Heath, Romford RM6 4XT. Tel: (0181) 559 5231. N, B.

Reid Kerr College, Renfrew Road, Paisley PA3 4DR. Tel: (0141) 889 4225. S, GS, SV.

Rhondda College, Llwynpia, Tonypandy CF40 2TQ. Tel: (01443) 432187. N, G, B.

Richmond Upon Thames Tertiary College, Egerton Road, Twickenham, Middx TW2 7SJ. Tel: (0181) 555 1422. N.

Rockingham College of FE, West Street, Wath Upon Dearne S63 6PX. Tel: (01709) 760310. N.

Rother Valley College, Doe Quarry Lane, Dinnington, Sheffield S31 8QH. Tel: (01909) 550550. N.

Rotherham College of Arts and Technology, Eastwood Lane, Rotherham S65 1EG. Tel: (01709) 362111. N, B.

Runshaw College, Langdale Road, Leyland, Lancs PR5 2DQ. Tel: (01772) 432511. N, G, B.

S

Salisbury College, Southampton Road, Salisbury SP1 2LW. Tel: (01722) 323711. N, G, B.

Sandwell College of Further and Higher Education, High Street, West Bromwich B70 8DW. Tel: (0121) 556 6000. N, G, B.

Selby College, Abbot's Road, Selby YO8 8AT. Tel: (01757) 702606. N, G, B.

Shetland College, Lerwick, Shetland ZE1 0BB. Tel: (01595) 5514. S, GS, SV.

Shrewsbury College, Radbrook Road, Shrewsbury SY3 9BL. Tel: (01743) 232686. N, G.

Solihull College, Blossomfield Road, Solihull B91 1SB. Tel: (0121) 711 2111. N, G.

Somerset College of Arts and Technology, Wellington Road, Taunton TA1 5AX. Tel: (01823) 283403. N, B.

Southgate College, High Street, London N14 6BS. Tel: (0181) 982 5423. N, B.

South Downs College of FE, College Road, Havant, Hants PO7 8AA. Tel: (01705) 257011. N, B.

South East Essex College of Arts & Technology, Carnarvon Road, Southend on Sea SS2 6LS. Tel: (01702) 220440. N, G, B.

South Cheshire College, Dane Bank Avenue, Crewe CW2 8AB. Tel: (01270) 69133. N, G, B, H.

South Devon College, Newton Road, Torquay TQ2 5BY. Tel: (01803) 217511. N, G, B, H.

South Kent College, Shorncliffe Road, Folkestone CT20 2NA. Tel: (01303) 850061. N, G, B.

South Trafford College, Manchester Road, West Timperley, Altrincham WA14 5PQ. Tel: (0161) 973 7064. N, G.

South Tyneside College, St Georges Avenue, South Shields NE34 6ET. Tel: (0191) 456 0403. N, G, B.

Southampton Technical College, St Mary Street, Southampton SO9 4WX. Tel: (01703) 635222. N, G, B.

Southport College, Mornington Road, Southport PR9 0TT. Tel: (01704) 500606. N, G, B.

St Austell College, Trevarthian Road, St Austell PL25 4BW. Tel: (01726) 67911. N, G.

St Helens College, Brook Street, St Helens WA10 1PZ. Tel: (01744) 33766. N, G, B.

Stafford College, Earl Street, Stafford ST16 2QR. Tel: (01785) 223800. N, G, B.

Stamford College, Melborne Road, Stamford, Lincs PE9 1XA. Tel: (01780) 64141. N, G, B.

Stoke on Trent College, Stoke Road, Shelton, Stoke on Trent ST4 2DG. Tel: (01782) 208208. N, G, B.

Stratford Upon Avon College, The Willows North, Alcester Road,

Stratford Upon Avon CV37 9QR. Tel: (01789) 266245. N, G, B.

Suffolk College, Rope Walk, Ipswich IP4 1LT. Tel: (01473) 255855. N, G, B.

Swansea College, Tycoch Road, Sketty, Swansea SA2 9EB. Tel (01792) 206871. N, G.

Swindon College, North Star Avenue, Swindon SN2 1DY. Tel: (01793) 498266. N, B.

T

Tameside College of Technology, Beaufort Road, Ashton Under Lyne OL6 6NX. Tel: (0161) 330 6911. N, G, B, H.

Tamworth College, Croft Street, Upper Gungate, Tamworth B79 8AE. Tel: (01827) 310202. N, B.

Telford College, Edinburgh EH4 2NZ. Tel: (0131) 332 0127. S, SV, HCIMA.

Telford College of Arts and Technology, Haybridge Road, Wellington, Telford TF1 2NP. Tel: (01952) 642200. N, G.

Thames Valley University, Wellington Street, Slough SL1 1YG. Tel: (01753) 697603. N, G, B, H.

Thanet College, Ramsgate Road, Broadstairs CT10 1PN. Tel: (01843) 865111. N, G, B.

The City College Manchester, 141 Barlow Moor Road, West Didsbury, Manchester M20 8PQ. Tel: (0161) 957 1500. N, G, B.

The Henley College, Deanfield Avenue, Henley on Thames RG9 1UH. Tel: (01491) 579988. N, G.

The Sheffield College, Granville Road, Sheffield S2 2RL. Tel: (01742) 760271. N, G, B, H.

Thomas Danby College, Roundhay Road, Leeds LS7 3BG. Tel: (0113) 2494912. N, G, B, H.

Thurrock College, Woodview, Grays, Essex RM16 4YR. Tel: (01375) 391199. N, G.

Thurso College, Ormlie Road, Thurso KW14 7EE. Tel: (01847) 83555. S, GS, SV.

Tresham Institute, George Street, Corby, Northants NN17 1QA. Tel: (01536) 402252. N, B.

Trowbridge College, College Road, Trowbridge, Wilts BA14 0ES. Tel: (01225) 766241. N.

W

Wakefield College, Margaret Street, Wakefield WF1 2DH. Tel: (01924) 370501. N, G, B.

Walsall College of Arts & Technology, St Paul's Street, Walsall WS1 1XN. Tel: (01922) 720824. N, G, B.

Waltham Forest College, Forest Road, London E17 4JB. Tel: (0181) 527 2311. N, G, B.

Weald College, Brookshill, Harrow Weald, Middx HA3 6RR. Tel: (0181) 954 9571. N, G.

Westminster College, Vincent Square, London SW1P 2PD. Tel: (0171) 828 1222. N, G, B, H.

West Cheshire College, Greenbank Centre, Eaton Road, Chester CH4 7ET. Tel: (01244) 677677. N, G, B.

West Cumbria College, Park Lane, Workington CA14 2RW. Tel: (01900) 64331. N, G, B.

West Herts College, Langley Road, Watford WD1 3RH. Tel: (01923) 240311. N, G, B.

West Lothian College, Bathgate EH48 1QJ. Tel: (01506) 634300. S, SV.

West Kent College, Brook Street, Tonbridge TN9 2PW. Tel: (01732) 358101. N, G, B, H.

West Nottinghamshire College, Derby Road, Mansfield NG18 5BH. Tel: (01623) 27191. N, G, B.

West Suffolk College, Out Risbygate, Bury St Edmunds IP33 3RL. Tel: (01284) 701301. N, G, B, H.

West Thames College, London Road, Isleworth, Middx TW7 4HS. Tel: (0181) 568 0244. N, G, B.

Weston College of FE, Knightstone Road, Weston Super Mare, Avon BS23 2AL. Tel: (01934) 411411. N, B.

Weymouth College, Newstead Road, Weymouth DT4 0DX. Tel: (01305) 208978. N, B.

Wigan and Leigh College, Parson's Walk, Wigan WN1 1RS. Tel: (01942) 494911. N, G, B.

Wirral Metropolitan College, Eastham L62 0AY. Tel: (0151) 327 4331. N, G, B, H.

Worcester College of Technology, Deansway, Worcester WR1 2JF. Tel: (01905) 723383. N, G, B, H.

Y

Yeovil College, Ilchester Road, Yeovil BA21 3BA. Tel: (01935) 23921.

York College of Further and Higher Education, Tadcaster Road, York YO2 1UA. Tel: (01904) 704141. N, G, B.

Yorkshire Coast College, Lady Edith's Drive, Scarborough YO12 5RN. Tel: (01723) 372105. N, G, B.

Ystrad Mynach College, Twyn Road, Hengoed, Ystrad Mynach CF8 7XR. Tel: (01443) 816888. N, G, B

EMPLOYERS: HOTEL GROUPS

Best Western Hotels, Vine House, 143 London Road, Kingston Upon Thames, Surrey KT2 6NA. Tel: (0181) 541 0050. An organisation representing 200 privately owned hotels.

Compass Hotels Ltd, Great Northern Hotel, Kings Cross, London N1 9AN. Tel: (0171) 283 4363.

Concord Hotels, 7 Green Road, Terriers, High Wycombe, Bucks HP13 5BD. Tel: (01494) 523906. 20 hotels in the south/south west.

Copthorne Hotels Ltd, Victoria House, Horley, Surrey RH6 7AF. Tel: (01293) 772288. 30 hotels Europe-wide.

De Vere Hotels, Chester Road, Daresbury, Warrington, Cheshire WA4 4BN. Tel: (01925) 265050.

Edwardian Hotels, 140 Bath Road, Hayes, Middx. Tel: (0181) 897 6644.

Forte (Forte Posthouse, Forte Crest, Forte Heritage, Forte Grand, Forte Exclusive Hotels of the World), St Martin's House, 20 Queensmere, Slough, Berks SL1 1YY. Tel: (01753) 573266.

Forte Travelodge: Unit 2, Cartell Business Centre, Stroudley Road, Basingstoke, Hants RG24 8FW. Tel: (01256) 330911. 800 hotels worldwide, including 350 in the UK.

Friendly Hotels Plc, Premier House, 10 Greycoat Place, London SW1P 1SB. Tel: (0171) 222 8866. 25 hotels in UK and Europe.

Hatton Hotels, Hatton Court, Upton St Leonard, Gloucester GL4 8DE.

Hilton UK, PO Box 137, Millbuck House, Clarendon Road, Watford, Herts WD1 1DN. Tel: (01923) 246464. 296 hotels worldwide.

Holiday Inn Crowne Plaza, Midland Hotel, Peter Street, Manchester M60 2DS.

Hyatt International Hotels, Cadogan Place, London SW1X 9PY.

ITT Sheraton Hotels, Bath Road, Hayes, Middx UB3 5BP.

Jarvis Hotels, Wye House, London Road, High Wycombe, HP11 1LH. Tel: (01494) 437800. 40 hotels in the UK.

Marriott - Scott's Hotels Ltd., Heathrow Marriott, Ditton Road, Langley, Berks SL3 8PT. Tel: (01753) 544255.

Marston Hotels, The Hythe Imperial, Princes Parade, Hythe, Kent CT21 6AE. Tel: (01303) 267441. 5 three and four star hotels in the UK.

Metropole Hotels, National Exhibition Centre, Birmingham B40 1PT. Tel: (0121) 780 4266.

Mount Charlotte Thistle Hotels, 2 The Calls, Leeds LS2 7JU. Tel: (0113) 2439111. 100 three and four star hotels in the UK.

Novotel Hotels, 1 Shartlands, Hammersmith, London W6 8DR. Tel: (0181) 741 1555.

Periquito Hotels, Riversdell House, Guildford Street, Chertsey, Surrey KT16 9AU. Tel: (01932) 570010.

Principal Hotel Group Plc, 11 Ripon Road, Harrogate, North Yorks HG1 2JA. Tel: (01423) 530797.

Queens Moat Houses Plc, Queens Court, 9-17 Eastern Road, Romford, Essex RM1 3NG. Tel: (01708) 730522.

Ramada International, Ramada International Heathrow, Bath Road, Hounslow, Middx TW6 2AQ. Tel: (0181) 750 2196.

Resort Hotels, Resort House, Edward Street, Brighton BN2 2HW. Tel: (01273) 676717.

Scottish Highland Hotels, 98 West George Street, Glasgow G2 1PW. Tel: (0141) 332 6538. 10 hotels in Scotland.

The Savoy Group of Hotels and Restaurants, 18 Brooks Mews, London W1Y 1LF. Tel: (0171) 499 4677.

Shire Inns Ltd, Colne Road, Reedley, Burnley, Lancs BB10 2NG. Tel: (01282) 414141. 8 hotels in the UK.

Stakis Hotels, 3 Atlantic Quay, York Street, Glasgow G2 8JH. Tel: (0141) 204 4321.

Swallow Hotels, PO Box 30, Parsons Road, Washington, Tyne & Wear NE37 1QS. Tel: (0191) 419 4545.

Whitbread Group of Hotels, Oakley House, Oakley Road, Luton, Beds LU4 9QH. Tel: (01582) 396922. 77 hotels and Travel Inns in the UK.

Tips

- Before making an application check whether it should be forwarded to the company's head office (as listed above) or the individual hotel you wish to work in.

- Also remember to apply to your local, privately owned hotels. Details of these can be found in your *Yellow Pages*.

EMPLOYERS: CATERING COMPANIES

Includes contract catering companies, fast food operators, restaurant chains and motorway service station operators.

ARA Services Plc, Beaumont House, 179-187 Arthur Road, London SW19 8AE. Tel: (0181) 944 9044. Contract catering.

Associated Catering Management Services, 1A Cranbourne Road, Slough, Berks SL1 2XF. Tel: (01753) 521719. Contract catering.

Bass Taverns, Hagley House, Hagley Road, Birmingham B16 8QG. Tel: (0121) 452 1911. Public houses.

Beefeater, PO Box 31, The Halfway House, Luton Road, Dunstable LU5

4AL. Tel: (01582) 660970. 275 restaurants and pubs in the UK.

Burger King Ltd, 20 Kew Road, Richmond, Surrey TW9 2NA. Tel: (0181) 332 2200. Fast food restaurants.

Capitol Catering Management Services Ltd, Orlin House, 5 Southern Court, South Street, Reading, Berks RG1 4QS. Tel: (01734) 560057. Contract catering.

Caterair UK Ltd., Saxby Court, 121-129 Victoria Road, Horley, Surrey RH6 9XG. Tel: (01293) 821036. In-flight catering.

Catering and Allied, Central House, Balfour Road, Hounslow, Middx TW3 1HA. Tel: (0181) 569 4343. Contract catering.

Compass Services (UK) Ltd., Queen's Wharf, Queen Caroline Street, London W6 6RJ. Tel: (0181) 741 1541. Contract catering.

Dominos Pizza, 10 Mayland Road, Tongwell, Milton Keynes MK15 8HF. Tel: (01908) 618222. Fast food.

Forte: *Welcome Break*, 2 Vantage Court, Tickford Street, Newport Pagnell, Bucks MK16 9EZ. Tel: (01908) 617766. 28 service stations in the UK and Germany.

Harvester, 1 David Road, Colnbrook, Slough SL3 0DB. Tel: (01753) 683636. 78 restaurants in the UK.

Little Chef: *Happy Eater*, Unit 2, Cartell Business Centre, Stroudley Road, Basingstoke, Hants RG24 8FW. Tel: (01256) 330911. 350 and 85 roadside restaurants respectively.

KFC, Colonel Sanders House, 88-97 High Street, Brentford, Middx TW8 8BG. Tel: (0181) 569 7070. 300 Kentucky Fried Chicken takeaways in the UK (80 are company owned, the remainder are owned by franchisees).

Gardner Merchant Ltd, Grant House, 114 Broadway, Salford, Manchester M5 2UW. Tel: (0161) 876 0705. Contract catering.

Granada Motorway Services Ltd., Toddington Service Area, Toddington, Beds LU5 6HR. Motorway service stations.

Groupe Chez Gerard Ltd, 33 Gresse Street, London W1P 1PN. Tel: (0171) 580 8788. Restaurants/wine bars in central London.

Leith's Good Food Ltd, 86 Bondway, London SW8 1SF. Tel: (0171) 735 6303. Contract and outside catering.

McDonald's Restaurants, 11-59 High Road, East Finchley, London N2 8AW. Tel: (0181) 883 6400. Fast food restaurants.

Pizza Express, 29 Wardour Street, London W1. Tel: (0171) 437 7215. Fast food catering.

Pizza Hut (UK) Ltd, One Imperial Place, Elstree Way, Borehamwood, Herts WD6 1JN. Tel: (0181) 732 9000. 219 fast food restaurants in the UK.

Quadrant, Contract House, Faraday Road, Swindon SN3 5HQ. Contract catering.

Rank Motorway Services Ltd., 439-445 Godstone Road, Whyteleafe, Surrey CR3 0YG. Tel: (01883) 623355. Motorway service stations.

Roadchef Ltd, 41-47 Longsmith Street, Gloucester GL1 2HJ. Tel: (01452) 303373. Motorway service stations.

Russell and Brand Ltd, St Georges House, 2 Bromley Road, Beckenham, Kent BR3 2JE. Tel: (0181) 663 2220. Contract catering.

Shaw Catering Company Ltd, Dennis House, Hawley Road, Hinckley, Leics LE10 0PR. 200 contract catering sites in the UK.

Spud-U-Like, 34-38 Standard Road, London NW10 6EU. Tel: (0181) 965 0182. Fast food restaurants.

Sutcliffe Catering, Portland House, Aldermaston Court, Church Road, Aldermaston, Berks RG7 4XS. Tel: (01734) 810144. Contract catering.

Toby Restaurants, Portland Road Training Centre, Cape Hill Brewery, PO Box 27, Birmingham B16 0PQ. Tel: (0121) 558 1481. Restaurants.

Travellers Fare Ltd, 50 Paul Street, London EC2A 4AE. Tel: (0171) 729 2200. Cafes/fast food.

Whitbread Inns, Park Square Chambers, 14 Park Street, Luton LU1 3EP. Pubs/catering.

TIPS:

● Before making an application check whether it should be forwarded to the company's head office (as listed above) or to the individual branch you wish to work in.

● Also remember to apply to your local, privately owned restaurants and catering companies. Details of these can be found in your *Yellow Pages*.

OTHER USEFUL ADDRESSES

Academy of Wine Service, Five Kings House, 1 Queen Street Place, London EC4R 1QS. Tel: (01483) 302373.

Brewer's Society, 423 Portman Square, London W1H 0BB. Tel: (0171) 486 4831.

British Association of Hotel Accountants (BAHA), PO Box 128, Edgware, Middx HA8 6TR. Tel: (0181) 952 0673.

British Hospitality Association, 40 Duke Street, London W1M 6HR. Tel: (0171) 499 6641.

British Institute of Innkeeping (BII), 51-53 High Street, Camberley, Surrey GU15 3RG. Tel: (01276) 684449.

British Tourist Authority (BTA), Thames Tower, Blacks Road, London W6 9EL. Tel: (0181) 846 9000.

BTEC (Business and Technology Education Council), Central House, Upper Woburn Place, London WC1H 0HH. Tel: (0171) 413 8400.

Caterer and Hotelkeeper Magazine, Quadrant House, The Quadrant, Sutton, Surrey SM2 5AS. Tel: (0181) 652 3500.

Catering Update and Caterer and Hotelkeeper Helpline (An enquiry and information service aiming to answer questions on any aspect of the hospitality business.) Tel: (01839) 373737. (Calls charged at premium rates).

Catering Managers Association (CMA), Kirby College of FE, Roman Road, Linthorpe, Middlesbrough, Cleveland TS5 5PJ. Tel: (01642) 813706.

Charles Forte Foundation, 166 Holborn, London WC1V 6TT. (Confers grants on suitable applicants wishing to study or undertake research in the hospitality industry.)

Chartered Institute of Marketing, Moor Hall, Cookham, Maidenhead, Berks SL6 9QH. Tel: (01628) 524922.

Chefs and Cooks Circle, PO Box 239, London N14 7NT.

City & Guilds of London Institute, 46 Britannia Street, London WC1X 9RG. Tel: (0171) 278 2468.

Confederation of Tourism, Hotel and Catering Management, 204 Barnett Wood Lane, Ashtead, Surrey KT21 2DB. Tel: (01372) 278572.

Cookery and Food Association, 1 Victoria Parade, Richmond, Surrey TW9 3NB. Tel: (0181) 948 3870.

Court of Master Sommeliers, 27 St Matthews Road, Chelston, Torquay, Devon TQ2 6JA. Tel: (01803) 605031.

English Tourist Board (ETB), Thames Tower, Blacks Road, London W6 9EL. Tel: (0181) 846 9000.

European Association of Hotel and Tourism Schools, Eastleigh College, Chestnut Avenue, Eastleigh, Hants SO4 5HT. Tel: (01703) 644011.

European Catering Association, 1 Victoria Parade, Richmond, Surrey TW9 3NB. Tel: (0181) 940 4464.

Hospital Caterers Association, Castle Hill Hospital, Castle Road, Cottingham, N Humberside HU16 5JQ. Tel: (01482) 875875.

Hotel, Catering and Institutional Management Association (HCIMA), 191 Trinity Road, London SW17 7HN. Tel: (0181) 672 4251.

Hotel and Catering Personnel and Training Association, 24 Chestnut Road, Twickenham, Middx TW2 5QZ. Tel: (0181) 894 1279.

Hotel and Catering Training Company (HCTC), International House, High Street, Ealing, London W5 5DB. Tel: (0181) 579 2400.

Hotel Career Centre, 43 Norwich Avenue West, Bournemouth BH2 6AJ. Tel: (01202) 291877.

Institute of Brewing, 33 Clarges Street, London W1Y 8EE. Tel: (0171) 499 8144.

Institute of Commercial Management, PO Box 125, Bournemouth BH2 6JH. Tel: (01202) 290999.

Institute of Hotel Security Management, c/o London Marriott Hotel, Grosvenor Square, London W1A 4AW. Tel: (0171) 493 1232.

International Flight Catering Association, 4 Grendon Close, Horley, Surrey RH6 8JW. Tel: (01293) 771872.

Local Authorities Caterers Association, 33 Grangefields Road, Jacobs Well, Guildford, Surrey GU4 7NR. Tel: (01483) 35523.

The Master Innholders, The Old Bakery, South Road, Reigate, Surrey RH2 7LU. Tel: (01737) 245195.

Mobile and Outside Caterers Association of Great Britain, 7 Hamilton Way, Wallington, Surrey SM6 9NJ. Tel: (0181) 669 8121.

National Association of Licensed House Managers, 9 Coombe Lane, London SW20 8NE. Tel: (0181) 946 3080.

National Federation of Fish Fryers, Federation House, 289 Dewsbury Road, Leeds LS11 5HW. Tel: (0113) 2713291.

National Licensed Victuallers Association (NVLA), Boardman House, 2 Downing Street, Farnham, Surrey GU9 7NX. Tel: (01252) 714448.

Northern Ireland Hotels & Caterers Association, 108/110 Midland Bank Building, Whitla Street, Belfast BT15 1JP. Tel: (01232) 351110.

Scottish Licensed Trade Association, 10 Walker Street, Edinburgh EH3 7LA. Tel: (0131) 225 5169.

Scottish Vocational Education Council (SCOTVEC), 24 Douglas Street, Glasgow G2 7NQ. Tel: (0141) 248 7900.

Society of Golden Keys, c/o Dukes Hotel, 35 St James's Place, London SW1A 1NY. Tel: (0171) 491 4840.

Springboard, 1 Denmark Street, London WC2H 8LP. Tel: (0171) 497 8654.

The University Catering Officers, c/o University of Dundee, Perth Road, Dundee DD1 4HN. Tel: (01382) 23181.

United Kingdom Bartenders Guild, 91-93 Gordon Road, Harborne, Birmingham B17 9HA. Tel: (0121) 427 8099.

United Kingdom Housekeepers Association, Flat 7, 14-15 Molyneux Street, London W1H 5HU. Tel: (0171) 723 6668.

Wine Guild of Great Britain, 190 Queen's Gate, London SW7 5EU. Tel: (0171) 584 9925.

Wine and Spirit Education Trust, Five Kings House, 1 Queen Street Place, London EC4R 1QS. Tel: (0171) 236 3551.

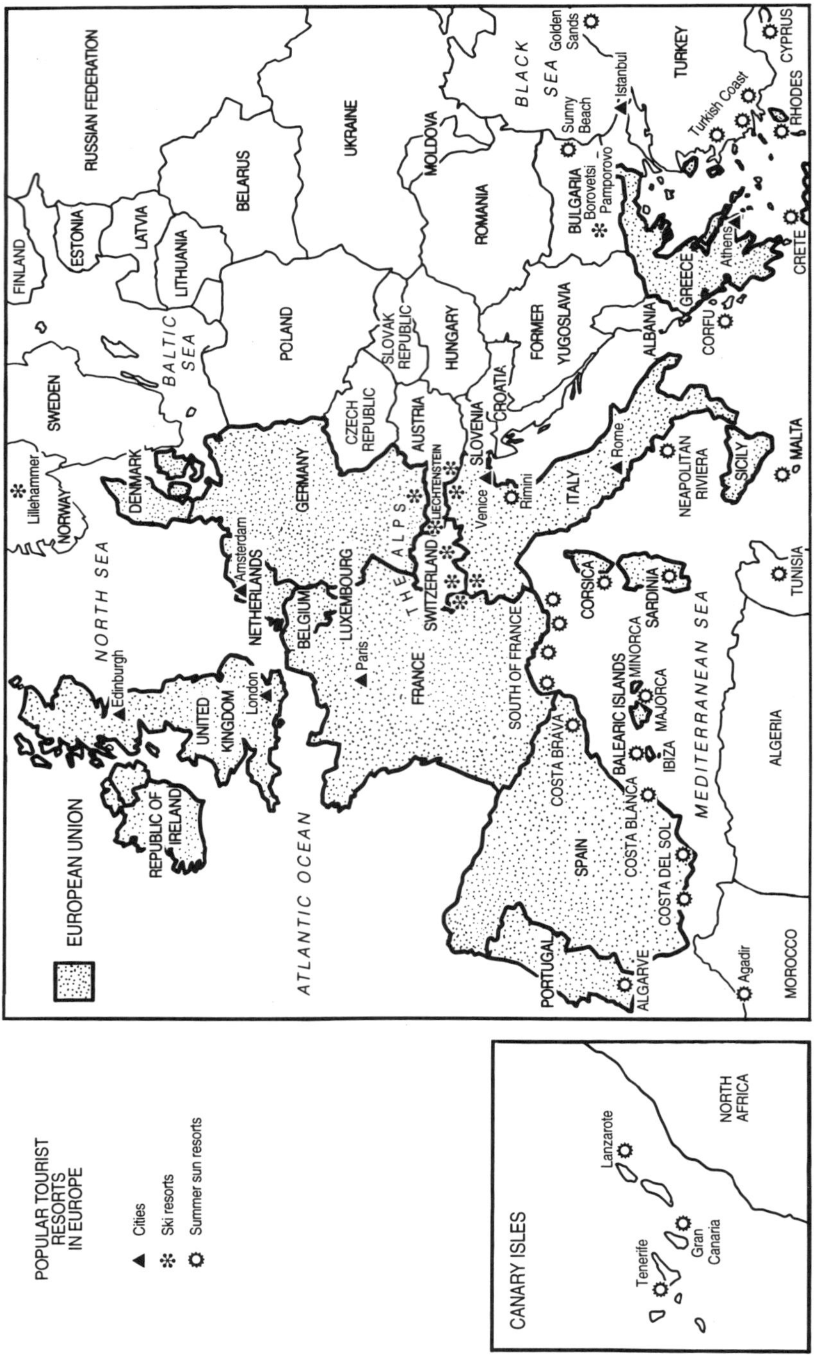

Fig. 8. Map of Europe and the Mediterranean area.

6
The Hotel and Catering Industry Worldwide

Advice for people wishing to work abroad

If you wish to work in hotels and catering abroad then use all the methods discussed in Chapter 4. In the rest of this chapter you will also find more useful information on employment, together with employment contacts, for many countries of the world.

If you are a student, or already have some experience in the hospitality industry, then a good way of getting work abroad is to go on an exchange or international work experience scheme. Many countries and organisations operate such schemes, allowing suitable applicants to spend a period working in hotels and catering abroad. These schemes are covered in this chapter.

EUROPE

The British Hospitality Association

The BHA administer the HOTREC stagiaire scheme, which offers working exchanges in the European Union. You must have 12 months' experience in the hospitality industry and a basic hospitality qualification, as a minimum. For details contact: British Hospitality Association, 40 Duke Street, London W1M 6HR. Tel: (0171) 499 6641.

The Young Workers Exchange Programme

The YWEP supports exchange schemes which provide up to 16 months' work experience in another European Union country for students or those who have training or experience in the hospitality industry (amongst others). The scheme is administered by the Central Bureau, but most schemes are organised through employers or colleges. Alternatively, it is possible to gain funding for an exchange scheme which you arrange yourself, through the Youth Exchange Programme. Central Bureau for Educational Visits and Exchanges, Seymour Mews House, Seymour Mews, London W1H 9PE. Tel: (0171) 486 5101.

France

About hotel and catering in France
France is one of the world's great countries for hotels and restaurants; the provision of hospitality is seen as an art, rather than an industry. Every French town has a huge selection of hotels and eating places, offering an extremely high standard of catering at modest prices.

The French view is very much that French food is the best in the world and only the French can cook it well. This attitude is slowly changing but there is still something of a resistance to foreign food and any sort of mass-produced catering, such as fast food hamburgers.

Types of work available
France offers opportunities in most of the types of work covered in Chapter 3. You must be very good to get any job, especially one in a restaurant.

Certain City & Guilds and SCOTVEC qualifications relating to some jobs in hospitality (receptionist, waiter, wine waiter, bar staff and chef) have an equivalent French qualification. However, most other jobs do not.

Sources to use
Write to potential employers in the first instance. Addresses of hotels, and some restaurants, can be obtained from tourist offices and chambers of commerce.

Vacancies are also advertised in the French newspapers and a small number in *Overseas Jobs Express.* Apart from the French newspapers there are some English language newspapers in the south of France.

Also use the French Job Centres. These are called ANPEs and are found in most French towns. They can only be used by personal callers. A special agency called CIDJ can advise young people on casual jobs in summer.

Private employment agencies operate in most towns. ECCO and Manpower have offices everywhere in France. See the French *Yellow Pages* (Pages Jaunes) for details; these are kept at larger libraries in the UK.

Some casual jobs can be had by just turning up and asking around at the start of the season, particularly in the south of France.

For further advice and contacts refer to *How to Get a Job in France*, published by How To Books.

Visas and permits
UK nationals do not need a visa or a work permit in order to get a job in France. However you will need a residence permit (called a Carte de Séjour) if you want to stay longer than three months. This can be obtained at the local town hall (known as the Mairie).

Other things you should know
Living costs in France are slightly lower than the UK, although accommodation is costly and hard to find in some places, especially the south and in Paris.

Most employers pay higher wages than the UK and there is a minimum national wage: 'le SMIC', about £5 per hour. Employers much prefer those who can speak at least a little French.

Useful contacts
Embassies
French Embassy, 58 Knightsbridge, London SW1X 7JT. Tel: (0171) 235 8030.
British Embassy, 35 rue de Faubourg St Honoré, 75008 Paris. Tel: 1 42 66 91 42.

Chambers of Commerce
Franco-British Chamber of Commerce, 197 Knightsbridge, London WC1V 6JJ. Tel: (0171) 831 9048.
Franco-British Chamber of Commerce, 8 rue Cimarosa, 75116 Paris.

Tourist Office in London
French Tourist Office, 178 Piccadilly, London W1V 0AL. Tel: (0171) 491 7622.

Tourist Authority
Ministère de Tourisme, 101 rue de Grenelle, 75007 Paris. Tel: 1 45 56 20 20.
Maison de la France, 8 avenue d'Opéra, 75001 Paris. Tel: 1 42 96 10 23.

Main Tourist Offices
127 avenue des Champs Elysées, 75008 Paris. Tel: 1 42 23 61 72.
place Bellcour, Lyon. Tel: 78 42 25 75.
4 la Canebière, Marseille. Tel: 91 54 91 11.

State Employment Service
ANPE, 53 rue Général Leclerc, 92136 Issy les Moulineaux.

Private Employment Agencies
ECCO, 33 rue Raffet, 75016 Paris. Tel: 1 45 25 51 51.
Kelly, 50 avenue des Champs Elysées, 75008 Paris. Tel: 1 42 56 44 88.
Manpower, 9 rue Jacques Bingen, 75017 Paris. Tel: 1 47 66 03 03.
Alpotels Agency, PO Box 388, London SW1X 8LW.

Newspapers
Le Monde, *Le Figaro* and *France-Soir* are the main national (Paris based) newspapers. Main regional newspapers are *Sud-Ouest* (Bordeaux), *La Voix du Nord* (Lille), *Ouest-France* (Rennes), *Le Progrès* (Lyon), *La Provençal* and *La Meridional* (Marseille). English language newspapers are *The News*, *Dordogne Telegraph* and *Riviera Reporter*.

Language courses
Berlitz, 79 Wells Street, London W1A 3BZ. Tel: (0171) 637 0330.
Alliance Française, 6 Cromwell Place, London SW7 2JN. Tel: (0171) 723 6439.

Other contacts
CIDJ, 101 quai Branly, 75740 Paris.

Employers:
Sogerba Forte, BP316-90/92, Rue Baudin, 92304 Levallois Perret, Paris. Tel: 1 41 27 17 17. (A Forte company operating 52 motorway service areas and 4 hotels.)
Forte, 23 Place Vendome, 75001 Paris.

Some major hotels/groups
George V, 31 avenue George V, 75008 Paris. Tel: 1 47 23 54 00.
Hotel Plaza Athénée, 25 avenue Montaigne, 75008 Paris. Tel: 1 47 23 78 33.
Hotel de la Trémoille, 14 rue de la Trémoille, 75008 Paris. Tel: 1 47 23 43 20.
Concorde Hotels, 58 boulevard Gouvion St Cyr, 75017 Paris. Tel: 1 40 68 52 92.
Le Meridien Hotels, 171 boulevard Haussmann, 75008 Paris. Tel: 1 44 20 52 00.
Novotel Hotels, 2 rue de la Mare Neuve, 91021 Evry Cedex. Tel: 1 60 77 04 58.

Work Experience Schemes
British Hospitality Association, 40 Duke Street, London W1M 6HR. Tel: (0171) 499 6641.

Central Bureau for Educational Visits and Exchanges, Seymour Mews House, Seymour Mews, London W1H 9PE. Tel: (0171) 486 5101.

Spain

About hotel and catering in Spain
Spain is one of the most popular tourist countries so far as British people are concerned. This has given rise to a substantial number of new hotels and catering outlets in Spain, although the massive expansion of the industry has now slowed down.

The most developed areas are the Costa Brava, Costa Blanca and Costa del Sol. The Balearic islands in the Mediterranean and the Canary Islands in the north Atlantic are also popular tourist spots. Elsewhere the hospitality industry is still quite underdeveloped.

Types of work available
Although all jobs in hotels and catering in Spain are open to all EU citizens, most British people tend to work in the very large package holiday industry. This is largely confined to casual work in hotels, restaurants, pubs, bars etc. Very few qualified people move to Spain at the moment.

A majority of the UK package tour operators operate to Spain but very few of them actually employ their own hotel and catering staff, so apply locally.

Sources to use
Those seeking work in Spain are advised to contact employers direct in the first instance. Recruitment for most summer jobs commences between November and January. Some vacancies are also advertised in *Overseas Jobs Express* and the Spanish newspapers. There are some English language newspapers in the main resort areas.

Other than this it is extremely difficult to locate vacancies from the UK. Those with experience should register with the OPU. The Spanish national employment service, CNC, is rarely able to place foreigners.

Visas and permits
UK nationals do not need a visa or a work permit in order to get a job in Spain. However, you will need an official residence permit (called a Residencia) if you wish to stay longer than three months. This can be obtained at main police stations.

Other things you should know
Spain offers low living costs, especially out of the main resorts, al-

though rates of pay are also lower than the UK. Those looking for work should remember there is much competition, especially from Spanish people who travel from areas of high unemployment to the resorts to look for work. As English is widely spoken in tourist resorts a knowledge of Spanish is not usually essential, although an advantage.

Useful contacts
Embassies
Spanish Embassy, 24 Belgrave Square, London SW1X 8QA. Tel: (0171) 235 5555.
British Embassy, Calle de Fernando el Santo 16, Madrid 4. Tel: 91 319 0200.

Chambers of Commerce
British Chamber of Commerce, Marques de Valdeiglas 3, Madrid 4.

Tourist Office in London
Spanish National Tourist Office, 57-58 James Street, London SW1. Tel: (0171) 499 0901.

Tourist Authority
SNTO, Veláquez 47, 28001 Madrid. Tel: 91 275 5603.

Main Tourist Offices
Gran Via 658, Barcelona.
Torre de Madrid, Plaza Espana, Madrid. Tel: 91 241 2325.
Avenida Rey Jaime III 10, Palma de Mallorca.
Avenida de la Constitución 21, Seville. Tel: 95 422 1404.

State Employment Service
CNC, General Pardinas 5, Madrid.

Private Employment Agencies
Restricted by law. Those which operate tend to handle mostly executive jobs.

Newspapers
El Pais, Diario 16 (Madrid), *El Diario de la Costa del Sol* (Malaga), *El Correo de Andalucia* (Seville). English language newspapers include *Sur in English, Costa Blanca News, Iberian Daily Sun.*

Language courses
Berlitz, 79 Wells Street, London W1A 3BZ. Tel: (0171) 637 0330.
Spanish Institute, 102 Eaton Square, London SW1. Tel: (0171) 235 1484.

Other contacts
The Hispanic and Luzo Brazilian Council, 2 Belgrave Square, London SW1X 8PJ.
Ministerio de Educacion y Cienca, Subdireccion General de Titulos, Convalidaciones y Homologaciones, Calle Alaca 34, 28014 Madrid. (Arranges for foreign qualifications to be recognised, where appropriate.)

Some major hotels/groups
Hotel Ritz, Plaza de la Lealtad 5, Madrid 280514. Tel: 91 521 2857.
Melia Hotels, Calle Princessa 27, 28008 Madrid. Tel: 91 241 8200.
Keytel International, Rambia de Cataluna 33, 08007 Barcelona. Tel: 93 301 3434.
Novotels, Calle Albacete 1, 28037 Madrid. Tel: 91 405 4600.
Santos Hotels, Calle Juan Bravo 8, Madrid. Tel: 91 431 2137.
Sol Group, Calle Gremio Toneleros 42, 07009 Palma de Mallorca. Tel: 971 298966.

Work Experience Schemes
British Hospitality Assocaition, 40 Duke Street, London W1M 6HR. Tel: (0171) 499 6641.
Central Bureau for Educational Visits and Exchanges, Seymour Mews House, Seymour Mews, London W1H 9PE. Tel: (0171) 486 5101.
TIVE, Oficina Nacional de Intercambio y Turismo de Jovenes y Estudiantes, José Ortega y Gasset 71, 28006 Madrid.

Greece

About hotel and catering in Greece
In ten years Greece has become the second most popular destination for British holidaymakers. It also attracts large numbers of Germans and Scandinavians. Over that time the tourist industry has changed completely. Hot weather, good beaches and nightlife now attract more visitors than the classical sites.

In spite of this the hospitality industry is still very underdeveloped. Most hotels and catering operations are individual, family owned concerns, which makes it quite difficult to find a job.

Types of work available

The openings are mostly restricted to hotel entertainments staff, restaurant cooks and waiting staff, and bar/nightclub staff in the tourist resorts. The most popular tourist islands are Corfu, Crete, Rhodes and Kos. Athens is also a major tourist centre.

A majority of the UK holiday companies offer a programme to Greece, but only a very small number employ any hotel and catering staff.

Sources to use

It can be difficult to find work in Greece due to the word-of-mouth way in which work is traditionally found. Visiting the country is probably the best way to find a job.

Those looking to pre-arrange jobs should look in the *Overseas Jobs Express* newspaper. There are also some English language newspapers in Athens which carry job vacancies.

There are a growing number of private employment agencies in Greece which are able to offer hotel and catering work. However, some of them may be unreliable in that the promised job is not available on arrival.

Visas and permits

UK nationals do not need a visa or a work permit in order to get a job in Greece. However, you will need a residence permit if you wish to stay longer than three months. This can be obtained at the local police station or, in Athens, at the Ministry of Public Order.

Other things you should know

Greece has a very low cost of living, but wages are also much lower than the UK. Many employers prefer to recruit staff on a casual/unofficial basis and may not always be reliable about paying wages.

Useful contacts
Embassies
Greek Embassy, 1A Holland Park, London W11 3TP. Tel: (0171) 727 8040.
British Embassy, 1 Ploutarchou Street, Athens 10675. Tel: 01 723 6211.

Chambers of Commerce
British Hellenic Chamber of Commerce, 4 Valaritou Street, Athens 10450.

Tourist Authority
EOT - Greek National Tourist Organisation, Odos Amerikis 2B, 10564 Athens. Tel: 01 322 3111.

Tourist Office in London
Greek Tourist Office, 4 Conduit Street, London W1. Tel: (0171) 734 5997.

Main Tourist Offices
Syntagma Square, Athens. Tel: 01 324 1884.

State Employment Service
OAED, Thakris 8, 16610 Glyfada, Athens. Tel: 01 993 2589.

Private Employment Agencies
Camenos International Staff Consultancy, 12 Botsai Street, Athens 147.
Galentinas European Consultancy, PO Box 511181, 14510 Kifissia, Athens. Tel: 01 808 1005.
Intertom Agency, 24-26 Halkokondili Street, Athens 10432. Tel: 01 532 9470.
Pioneer, 11 Nikis Street, Athens 10557. Tel: 01 322 4321.

Newspapers
The *Athens News* and *Athens Daily Post* are English language news-papers.

Language courses
Linguaphone, 124 Brompton Road, London SW3 2TL. Tel: 0800 282417.

Other contacts
DEKASTA, Leof. Syngrou 56, 11742 Athens. Tel: 01 922 2526. (Advises on the acceptability of qualifications from other countries.)

Some major hotels/groups
Astir Hotels, 12 Praxitelous, 12400 Athens. Tel: 01 324 3961.

Work Experience Schemes
British Hospitality Association, 40 Duke Street, London W1M 6HR. Tel: (0171) 499 6641.
Central Bureau for Educational Visits and Exchanges, Seymour Mews House, Seymour Mews, London W1H 9PE. Tel: (0171) 486 5101.

Italy

About hotel and catering in Italy
Italy is the home of good hospitality, and a country where food is treated with great importance. The Italian hospitality industry is well developed, especially in the north of the country, but very much Italian in style. Foreign food and methods of service are quite rare; an Italian pizza takeaway is a totally different operation to that which you would find in the UK or USA!

Types of work available
Those who speak good Italian may be able to find jobs in all the categories discussed in Chapter 3. However, the majority of British workers in Italy find work in the hotels and restaurants in the Alpine ski resorts (such as Courmayeur and Sauze d'Oulx) which operate between November and April. However, the opportunities are not as great as in the other Alpine resorts as many Italians who work in the summer holiday resorts move to the ski resorts in the winter.

Sources to use
Those who speak some Italian should use the state employment agency, UCM. Newspapers are also a good source of vacancies for these people. There are no English language newspapers but the small ads magazine *Porta Portese* is useful for contacts and leads.

Applying direct to employers, whether by letter or in person, is recommended as much work in Italy is found in this way.

Visas and permits
UK nationals do not need a visa or a work permit in order to get a job in Italy. However, you will need a residence permit (called a Carta di Soggiorno di Cittadino di Uno Stato Membro della CEE) if you wish to stay longer than three months. This can be obtained at the local police station (Questura, Commissariato or Stazione di Carabinieri).

Other things you should know
The cost of living and wages are quite high in northern Italy, but rather lower in the south, where unemployment is a problem. A knowledge of Italian is desirable if not essential for anyone wishing to work in Italy.

Useful contacts
Embassies
Italian Embassy, 14 Three Kings Yard, London W1Y 2EH. Tel: (0171) 269 8200.

British Embassy, 80 Via Venti Settembre, 00100 Rome.

Chambers of Commerce
Italian Chamber of Commerce for Great Britain, 422 Walmar House, 296 Regent Street, London W1R 6AE. Tel: (0171) 637 3153.
British Chamber of Commerce, Courso Buenos Aires 77, 20124 Milan.

Tourist Office in London
1 Prince's Street, London W1R 8AY. Tel: (0171) 408 1254.

Tourist Authority
ENIT, Via Marghera 2, 00185 Rome. Tel: 06 49711.

Main Tourist Offices
Via Parigi 5, Rome. Tel: 06 463748.
Piazza San Marco, Venice. Tel: 041 715555.
Via Cavour 1, Florence. Tel: 055 278785.

State Employment Service
Ufficio di Collocamento Mandopera, Via Pastrengo 16, Rome.

Private Employment Agencies
Not permitted in Italy.

Newspapers
Il Messaggero, *Corriere della Sera*, *La Repubblica*, *La Voce Repubblicana* (Rome), *La Nazione* (Florence), *Corriere della Serra*, *Il Giornale* (Milan), *La Stampa* (Turin), *Il Giornale di Napoli* (Naples), *Il Gazzetino* (Venice).

Language courses
Berlitz, 79 Wells Street, London W1A 3BZ. Tel: (0171) 637 0330.
Inlingua, 8-10 Rotton Park Road, Birmingham B16 9JJ. Tel: (0121) 454 0204.

Other contacts
Servizio Turistico Sociale, via Zanetti 18, 50123 Florence. (Can often advise young people on short-term work opportunities and on exchanges.)

Some major hotels/groups
AGIP Forte International, Via Valentino Mazola 66, 00142 Rome. 18 hotels in Italy and Hungary.

Selected hotels
Via M.E. Lepido 203/14, 40132 Bologna. Tel: 051 401130.
Autosole Uscita Firenze Nord, 50013 Florence. Tel: 055 421 1881.
Tangenziale Ovest, 20090 Assago, Milan. Tel: 02 488 0441.
SS1 Via Aurelia, 00165 Rome. Tel: 06 637 9001.
Ingressa Autostrada TO/MI, 10036 Settimo Torinese, Turin. Tel: 011
    800 1855.
Rotonda Romea 1. CP 4129, 30175 Marghera, Venice. Tel: 041
    936900.
Forte Hotel Village, Santa Margherita di Pula, 09010 Cagliari, Sardi-
    nia. Tel: 070 921516.
Atahotels, Via Lampedusa 11/A, 20141 Milan. Tel: 02 895262.
Ciga Hotels, Via M. Barozzi 1, 20122 Milan. Tel: 02 68661.
Italhotels, Via Sacchi 8, 10128 Turin. Tel: 011 542950.
Jolly Hotels, Via Bellini 6, 36078 Valdagno. Tel: 0445 410000.

Work Experience Schemes
British Hospitality Association, 40 Duke Street, London W1M 6HR.
    Tel: (0171) 499 6641.
Central Bureau for Educational Visits and Exchanges, Seymour Mews
    House, Seymour Mews, London W1H 9PE. Tel: (0171) 486 5101.

Portugal

About hotel and catering in Portugal
The hotel and catering industry in Portugal is still one of the least
developed in Europe; there are no large groups as in the UK. However, there is a growing tourist industry, particularly in the southern
province of the Algarve, where there are many hotels, apartment complexes, restaurants and bars.
    As well as the Algarve the capital Lisbon, and its nearby resort of
Estoril, together with the Portuguese island of Madeira, in the Atlantic
Ocean, are popular tourist areas.

Types of work available
The fact that a great deal of tourism is based on self-catering accom-
modation reduces the job opportunities, especially for foreigners.
Most opportunities are casual jobs in restaurants, bars etc.

Sources to use
Apply direct to employers in the first instance — by written, telephone or personal application to local Portuguese employers. Newspapers offer some vacancies and there are several English language

newspapers in Lisbon, the Algarve and one in Madeira. A very small number of vacancies arise in the *Overseas Jobs Express*; other than this, few jobs in Portugal are advertised as such. Few employment agencies offer jobs of this type.

Visas and permits
UK nationals do not need a visa or a work permit in order to get a job in Portugal. However, you will need a residence permit (called a Residência) if you wish to stay longer than three months. This can be obtained at the local Serviçio de Estrangeiros (Alien Registration Office).

Other things you should know
Portugal offers a low cost of living together with lower wages than the UK. It is not essential to speak Portuguese to get most jobs in the tourist industry. As employment of EU citizens has only very recently been permitted, many employers are not yet used to employing non-Portuguese workers.

Useful contacts
Embassies
Portuguese Embassy, 11 Belgrave Square, London SW1X 8PP. Tel: (0171) 235 5331.
British Embassy, Rua de S. Domingos à Lapa, 1200 Lisbon. Tel: 01 396 1191.

Chambers of Commerce
British-Portuguese Chamber of Commerce, Rua de Estrela 8, 1200 Lisbon.

Tourist Office in London
1-5 New Bond Street, London W1Y 0NP. Tel: (0171) 493 3873.

Tourist Authority
IPT, Rua Alexandre Herculana 51, 1127 Lisbon. Tel: 01 847 3071.

Main Tourist Offices
Praço do Restauradores, Lisbon. Tel: 01 571745.
Rua da Misericórdia, Faro, Algarve.
Largo Marquês de Pombal, Lagos, Algarve.

State Employment Service
Ministério de Trabalho, Praça de Londres, 1091 Lisbon Codex.

Private Employment Agencies
Do not usually offer seasonal work in hotels/catering. Robert Shaw & Associates, Rua Sampaio E Pina 70-10, 1000 Lisbon, deals in some senior management positions.

Newspapers
Correio de Manha, O Diario, Diario de Noticias, Jornal O Dia (Lisbon), *Jornal de Noticias* (Oporto).
English language newspapers include *Portugal Post, Algarve News, Anglo-Portuguese News* and *Madeira Island Bulletin.*

Language courses
Linguaphone, 124 Brompton Road, London SW3 2TL. Tel: 0800 282417.
Portuguese Language School, PO Box 70, London SW15. Tel: (0181) 877 1738.

Other contacts
The Hispanic and Luzo Brazilian Council, 2 Belgrave Place, London SW1X 8PJ.
The following organisations can advise on casual work opportunities and exchanges for young people:
Associacão de Turismo Estudantil e Juvenil, Box 4586, 4009 Oporto.
Instituto da Juventude, Avenida da Liberdade 194, 1200 Lisbon.
Ministério da Juventude, Estrada das Laranjeiras 197/205, 1600 Lisbon. Tel: 01 726 5552.

Some major hotels/groups
Hotel Dona Filipa, Vale do Lobo, 8136 Almansil, Algarve. Tel: 089 394141.
Penina Golf & Resort Hotel, PO Box 146, Penina, Algarve. Tel: 082 415415.

Work Experience Schemes
British Hospitality Association, 40 Duke Street, London W1M 6HR. Tel: (0171) 499 6641.
Central Bureau for Educational Visits and Exchanges, Seymour Mews House, Seymour Mews, London W1H 9PE. Tel: (0171) 486 5101.

Germany

About hotel and catering in Germany
Germany has a very well-developed hotel and catering industry,

which is at a similar level of development to that in the UK, although family-owned establishments are still popular. Several UK companies, including Forte and their Welcome Break division, have business interests in Germany.

A very important point to note about Germany is that the industry is not popular as a career choice for German workers. There is a shortage of manpower in some areas and this boosts the employment prospects compared with most other countries.

Germany has very few seaside resorts as such. Apart from the cities there are extensive hotel and catering facilities in the spa towns where Germans go to relax and use the spa baths. The most popular tourist regions are Bavaria and Baden-Wurtemburg, and the German Alpine resorts are popular with skiers. Much has been said about exploiting tourism in the former East Germany, but this has been developed very little at present.

Types of work available

There is no reason why those who speak fluent German should not be able to compete for any of the jobs discussed in Chapter 3. UK qualifications are often accepted by employers in several areas, including the City & Guilds in reception, waiting, chef and bar staff occupations.

Sources to use

The recruitment network in Germany is very well organised and all the methods discussed in Chapter 4 can be used. The state employment service, Arbeitsamt, is generally very helpful to foreigners and has a special bureau, called ZAV, which will deal with enquiries from the UK. However, private employment agencies are largely prohibited. Those who can speak German and offer a skill should register with the Overseas Placing Unit.

Most German national and regional newspapers carry a good selection of vacancies. However, few vacancies in Germany find their way into the UK press.

Writing to employers in search of a vacancy can be successful in Germany. Many employers who have difficulty in recruiting staff locally will make offers to those from abroad. Recruiting for casual summer jobs starts in February-March. Personal calling can also work, although the local Arbeitsamt will usually know of all the local vacancies.

Visas and permits

UK nationals do not need a visa or a work permit in order to get a job in Germany. However, you will need a residence permit (called an Aufenthaltserlaubnis) if you wish to stay longer than three months. This can be obtained at the local town hall (known as the Rathaus). To work in catering jobs you will need a health check and health certificate. This can be obtained at the local Gesundheitsamt.

Other things you should know

German wages are higher than in the UK, but German employers can be very demanding. Rigorous standards of safety, health and hygiene operate. Living costs are a little higher than in the UK. Although many Germans speak a little English a knowledge of German is really essential.

Useful contacts

Embassies

German Embassy, 23 Belgrave Square, London SW1X 0PZ. Tel: (0171) 235 5033.

British Embassy, Friedrich-Ebert-Allee 77, 5300 Bonn. Tel: 0228 234061.

Chambers of Commerce

German Chamber of Industry and Commerce, 16 Buckingham Gate, London SW1E 6LB. Tel: (0171) 233 5656.

British Chamber of Commerce in Germany (BCCG), Heumarkt 14, 5000 Cologne 1.

Tourist Office in London

61 Conduit Street, London W1R 0EN. Tel: (0171) 734 2600.

Tourist Authority

DZT, Beethovenstrasse 67, 6000 Frankfurt Am Main 1. Tel: 069 75720.

Main Tourist Offices

Europa Centre, Budapester Strasse, Berlin. Tel: 030 262 6031.
Hauptbahnhof, Frankfurt. Tel: 069230 5113.
Hauptbahnhof, Munich. Tel: 089 239 1256.
Klett Passage, Stuttgart. Tel: 0711 221453.

State Employment Service

Arbeitsamt, in most towns, but foreigners should contact ZAV, Feuerbachstrasse 42, 6000 Frankfurt Am Main.

Private Employment Agencies
Mostly prohibited by law. However some temporary work bureaux, such as Manpower, are permitted.

Newspapers
Frankfurter Allgemeine Zeitung, Die Welt (Frankfurt), *Süddeutsche Zeitung, Bayernkurier* (Munich), *Kölnsiche Rundschau* (Cologne), *Weser Kurier* (Bremen), *Stuttgarter Zeitung* (Stuttgart), *Berliner Morgenpost* (Berlin).

Language courses
Berlitz, 79 Wells Street, London W1A 3BZ. Tel: (0171) 637 0330.
Goethe Institute, 50 Prince's Gate, London SW7 2PH. Tel: (0171) 581 3344.

Other contacts
Alpotels Agency, PO Box 388, London SW1X 8LX. (Jobs in winter ski resorts.)
Deutsche Baderverband (Spa Resorts Association), Schumannstrasse 111, 5300 Bonn 1. (Information on facilities in spa towns.)
Deutscher Alpenverein e.V., Praterinsel 5, 8000 Munich 2. (Information on facilities in ski resorts).
Verband Deutscher Freizeitunternehmen e.V., Mittlerer Steinbachweg 2, 8700 Würzberg. (Information on holiday centres.)

Some major hotels/groups
Arabella Hotels, Arabellastrasse 5, 8000 Munich 81. Tel: 089 9232 4444.
Arcade Hotels, Mauritiusstrasse 5, 6200 Weisbaden. Tel: 0611 39361.
Atlantic Hotels, An der Alster 72, Hamburg 1. Tel: 040 28880.
Excelsior Hotels, Domplatz, Trankgasse 1, Cologne. Tel: 0221 2701.
Hotel Berlin, Lützowplatz 17, 1000 Berlin 30. Tel: 030 26050.
Kempinski Hotels, Am Forthaus Gravenbruch 9-11, 6078 Frankfurt/Neu Isenburg 2. Tel: 06102 51562.
Penta Hotels, Einemstrasse 24, 1000 Berlin 30. Tel: 02 500930.
Ringhotels, Belfortstrasse 8, 8000 Munich 80. Tel: 089 5959.
Romantik Hotel, Schlossstr. 4, Mannheim. Tel: 06202 26066.

Work Experience Schemes
British Hospitality Association, 40 Duke Street, London W1M 6HR. Tel: (0171) 499 6641.
Central Bureau for Educational Visits and Exchanges, Seymour Mews House, Seymour Mews, London W1H 9PE. Tel: (0171) 486 5101.

Switzerland

About hotel and catering in Switzerland
Much that has been said about Germany (see 'Germany') also applies
to Switzerland. The country has a very well developed hospitality
industry. Standards are very high. Many hotels and catering establishments have a difficulty in filling their vacancies.

Switzerland attracts a large number of tourists, but to the winter ski
resorts rather than in summer. The skiing season operates from No-
vember-April, depending on the weather. The main resorts are Davos,
Grindelwald, Gstaad, Klosters, St Moritz, Verbier and Zermatt.

Types of work available
Most British workers in Switzerland work in the winter skiing industry. Casual staff are required in hotels, restaurants and bars. This
includes qualified chefs, waiters and hotel staff, as well as those looking for casual work. It is much harder to find permanent full-time jobs.

Sources to use
The best way of finding work in Switzerland is to apply direct to
employers — write, telephone or call in person. The Jobs in the Alps
Agency has a number of jobs available each year and some seasonal
vacancies are advertised in *Overseas Jobs Express*.

You should also apply to UK ski holiday companies as several of
them run their own chalets and hotels and employ hotel and catering
staff in the UK. More information on this and contacts are given in
How to Get a Job in Travel and Tourism, available in this series.

Foreigners cannot generally use the Swiss national employment
service and few private employment agencies deal with travel and
tourism jobs. Local newspapers are of some limited use.

Visas and permits
Swiss employers are allocated a number of combined visa and work/
residence permits which they can give out to foreign workers of their
choice, rather than the employee having to apply for the permit as
elsewhere. However, the numbers are limited and so finding work depends not only on finding an employer but also on finding one with
permits available. A fair number of casual staff do work without permits, which is illegal.

As Switzerland has recently agreed with the European Union (of
which Switzerland is not a member) to relax these controls these permits may be abolished in the near future. You are advised to check
the current situation with the Embassy.

Other things you should know
Switzerland is an extremely expensive country in which to live. Accommodation can be very expensive and hard to find. Wages are high by UK standards and even casual work, such as dishwashing, can pay £200 per week.

Switzerland has three official languages (French, German and Italian) depending on the area, or canton, in which you are working. A knowledge of one of these is an advantage but not always essential.

Useful contacts
Embassies
Swiss Embassy, 16-18 Montagu Place, London W1H 2BQ. Tel: (0171) 723 0701.
British Embassy, Thunstrasse 50, 3000 Berne. Tel: 031 445021.

Chambers of Commerce
British-Swiss Chamber of Commerce, Freiestrasse 155, 8032 Zurich.

Tourist Office in London
Swiss Centre, 1 New Coventry Street, London W1V 3HG. Tel: (0171) 734 1921.

Tourist Authority
Swiss National Tourist Office, Bellariastrasse 38, 8027 Zurich. Tel: 01 2881111.

Main Tourist Offices
Gare Cornavin, Geneva. Tel: 022 731 6450.
Bahnhofplatz 15, Zurich. Tel: 01 482 3544.
Schifflande 15, Basle.
Bahnhof, Berne.

Newspapers
Neue Zuricher Zeitung (Zurich), *Basler Zeitung, Baslerstab* (Basle), *Berner Zeitung, Berner Tagwacht* (Berne), *La Suisse, La Tribune de Genève, Journal de Genève* (Geneva).

Language courses
The official languages of Switzerland are French, German and Italian. See relevant country sections for details of language courses.

Other contacts
Jobs in the Alps Agency, PO Box 388, London SW1X 8LX. (Employment agency.)

Some major hotels/groups
Brogosa AG, Via Gabietta, 6614 Brissago. Tel: 093 652766.
Hotel des Bergues, 33 Quai des Bergues, 1201 Geneva. Tel: 022 731 5050.
Hotel Zurich, Neumühlequal 42, 8001 Zurich. Tel: 01 363 6363.
Mövenpick Hotels International, Zurichstrasse 106, 8134 Adliswil. Tel: 01 812 2222.

Work Experience Schemes
A programme is operated in association with the Swiss Hotels Association. For details contact the British Hospitality Association, 40 Duke Street, London W1M 6HR. Tel: (0171) 499 6641.

Austria

About hotel and catering in Austria
The scope for foreign workers in Austria is quite limited as, like Switzerland, it is not part of the European Union. A knowledge of Austrian German, or at least German, is necessary.
    A large tourist industry operates, but mostly in the winter ski resorts. The main resorts are Kitzbühel, St Anton and Lech.

Types of work available
Many but not all UK ski package tour operators have a programme in the Austrian ski resorts. They require a small number of hotel, chalet, maintenance and entertainment staff. Other than this most jobs are of the casual type, particularly in bars and restaurants.

Sources to use
To pre-arrange work apply to the UK package tour companies. Details are given in the book *How to Get a Job in Travel and Tourism*, available in this series. A small number of seasonal vacancies are advertised in the *Overseas Jobs Express* in the autumn and winter.
    Casual jobs can sometimes be found by visiting Austria. Newspapers are of limited use. The state employment agency Landesarbeitsamt can help. Tourist offices sometimes know of vacancies.

Visas and permits
You will need a work permit in order to work legally in Austria. This

can only be obtained by your employer once a job has been found; the employee must not be in Austria at the time. A number of seasonal workers do work without permits, which is illegal.

Other things you should know
The cost of living and wages offered in Austria are significantly higher than in the UK, although not as high as in Switzerland. A knowledge of Austrian German is desirable; this is quite different from the German spoken in Germany.

Useful contacts
Embassies
Austrian Embassy, 18 Belgrave Mews West, London SW1X 8HU.
    Tel: (0171) 235 3731.
British Embassy, Jauresgasse 12, A-1010 Vienna. Tel: 01 713 1575.

Chambers of Commerce
Austrian Chamber of Commerce, Turkenstrasse 9, A-1090 Vienna.

Main Tourist Offices
Herrengasse 16, Graz. Tel: 0316 914076.
Kärntnerstrasse 38, Vienna. Tel: 0222 586 3246.

State Employment Services
Bebenbergerstrasse 33, A-8021 Graz.
Schöpfstrasse 5, Innsbruck.
Schiesstantstrasse 4, A-5021 Salzburg.
Hohenstauffengasse 2, A-1013 Vienna (Region).
Weihburggasse 30, Vienna (City).

Private Employment Agencies
Do not normally deal with work of this type.

Newspapers:
Die Press, Der Standard, Wiener Zeitung (Vienna), *Neue Tiroler Zeitung, Tiroler Tageszeitung, Salzburger Volkszeitung* (Salzburg).

Language courses
Berlitz, 79 Wells Street, London W1A 3BZ. Tel: (0171) 637 0330.
Further information available from the Anglo-Austrian Society, 46 Queen Anne's Gate, London SW1H 9AU. Tel: (0171) 222 0366.

Work Experience Schemes
Austrian Committee for the International Exchange of Students, (ÖKISTA), Türkenstrasse 4, A-1090 Vienna.

Belgium

About hotel and catering in Belgium
Belgium does not have a worldwide reputation for hospitality, but the Belgians regard this matter with the same importance as the French. The cuisine may not be as elaborate, but Belgian standards are still very high.

Opportunities can be found across the country, but the capital Brussels has most opportunities for foreigners, being a cosmopolitan and multilingual city.

Types of work available
All types of work as described in Chapter 3 are available to foreigners. Information on whether UK qualifications are acceptable to employers can be checked out with the local Chambre des Métiers et Négoces.

Sources to use
All the methods of finding work discussed in Chapter 4 can be used in Belgium. The state employment agency (called VDAB, FOREM or ONEM depending on the area) will help foreigners. Special T-Service bureaux offer temporary work, particularly in hotels and catering. Those with a language and skills to offer should register with the OPU.

Every Belgian town or city has a number of private employment agencies, such as ECCO. These can be located through the Belgian *Yellow Pages* and usually have plenty of temporary vacancies in hotels and catering.

Newspapers can be used for finding vacancies. Brussels has an excellent English language newspaper called *The Bulletin.*

Visas and permits
UK nationals do not need a visa or a work permit in order to get a job in Belgium. However, you will need a residence permit if you wish to stay longer than three months. This can be obtained at the local town hall.

Other things you should know
Belgium has a high standard of living. Living costs and wages are

slightly more than in the UK. In practical terms Belgium is divided into two — Wallonia in the south where French is spoken and Flanders in the north where Flemish (similar to Dutch) is spoken. The capital Brussels is midway between the two and is bilingual!

Useful contacts
Embassies
Belgian Embassy, 103 Eaton Square, London SW1Z 9AB.   Tel: (0171) 235 5422.
British Embassy, Britannia House, rue Joseph II 28, 1040 Brussels. Tel: 02 217 90 00.

Chambers of Commerce
Belgian-Luxembourg Chamber of Commerce, 6 John Street, London WC1N 2ES. Tel: (0171) 831 3508.
British Chamber of Commerce, Britannia House, rue Joseph II 30, 1040 Brussels. Tel: 02 219 07 88.

Tourist Authority
Office de Promotion de Tourisme, 61 rue Marché aux Herbes, 1000 Brussels. Tel: 02 504 02 00.

Main Tourist Offices
Hotel de Ville, Grand Place, 1000 Brussels. Tel: 02 513 8940.

State Employment Service
For Flanders: VDAB
For Wallonia: ONEM
Head office at boulevard de l'Empereur 7, 1000 Brussels.
In Brussels: ONEM, 38 rue d'Escalier, 1000 Brussels.
T-Service Bureau: 69 boulevard Anspach.

Private Employment Agencies
ECCO, 17a rue Vilian XIV, 1050 Brussels. Tel: 02 647 87 80.
Avenue Louise Interim, 207 avenue Louise, 1050 Brussels. Tel: 02 640 91 91.
Select Interim, 1-5 avenue de la Joyeuse Entrée, 1040 Brussels. Tel: 02 231 03 33.
Creyf's, 473 avenue Louise, 1050 Brussels. Tel: 02 646 34 34.

Newspapers
Le Soir (Brussels), *Antwerpse Morgan* (Antwerp), *La Meusse* (Liège).

In Brussels also see *Belgique No. 1* (free), *L'Echo* (free) and *The Bulletin* (English language).

Language courses
Berlitz, 70 Wells Street, London W1A 3BZ. Tel: (0171) 637 0330.
Inlingua, 8-10 Rotton Park Road, Birmingham B16 9JJ. Tel: (0121)
    454 0204.

Other contacts
Centre National Infor Jeunes, Impasse des Capucins 2/8, 5000 Namur.
    Tel: 081 22 08 72. — and 12 local offices in Belgium. (Can advise
    young people on study, exchanges, work, residence etc.)
Community Help Service (CHS), 102 rue St. Georges, PO Box 20,
    1050 Brussels. Tel: 02 647 67 80. (English speaking help and
    information service.)

Work Experience Schemes
British Hospitality Association, 40 Duke Street, London W1M 6HR.
    Tel: (0171) 499 6641.
Central Bureau for Educational Visits and Exchanges, Seymour Mews
    House, Seymour Mews, London W1H 9PE. Tel: (0171) 486 5101.

Netherlands

About hotel and catering in the Netherlands
The Netherlands has a very large and well developed hospitality
industry. In many ways it is similar to that in the UK, except that
there are still a large number of small, owner-operated establishments
— especially in the capital, Amsterdam. Standards are very high in all
areas of the industry.
    Several UK companies have interests in the Netherlands, and vice
versa. Catering and Allied contract caterers have a Dutch sister company,
Holland Catering Specialisten.

Types of work available
For those with some knowledge of Dutch most of the jobs discussed
in Chapter 3 can be considered. Casual work in hotels and catering
establishments is quite readily available (due to the very stringent
labour laws which relate only to permanent staff, employers are
enthusiastic about recruiting casual labour), and this is a good way to
start.

Sources to use
The job-finding network in the Netherlands is very well developed
and an agency is usually the best way of finding work.

Those with a knowledge of Dutch should register with the OPU.
The Netherlands employment service will help foreigners to find
work, but it is better to call on them in person. The Netherlands also
has a very large network of private employment agencies, known as
Uitzendbureaux, which can almost always offer some type of casual
work in hotel and catering.

Newspapers usually carry a large number of vacancies. However,
there are no suitable English language newspapers. Vacancies are
rarely advertised in the UK.

Approaching employers direct is also to be recommended and can
be done in person, by post, or by 'phone, as many employers speak at
least a little English.

Visas and permits
UK nationals do not need a visa or work permit in order to get a job
in the Netherlands. However, you will need a residence permit if you
wish to stay longer than three months. This can be obtained from a
main police station.

Other things you should know
Living costs are very similar to the UK; perhaps a little more for
some purchases. Wages are higher than in the UK and a legal minimum wage exists for all employees over 23. It should also be noted
that unemployment is higher than the UK in most places. Although
many people speak a little English, and some speak it fluently, a
knowledge of Dutch is preferred.

Useful contacts
Embassies
Royal Netherlands Embassy, 38 Hyde Park Gate, London SW7 5DP.
    Tel: (0171) 584 5040.
British Embassy, Lange Voorhout, The Hague 2514 ED. Tel: 070 364
    5800.

Chambers of Commerce
Dutch Chamber of Commerce, 307 High Holborn, London WC1. Tel:
    (0171) 405 1358.
Netherlands-British Chamber of Commerce, Javastraat 96, 2585 The
    Hague.

Tourist Authority
Netherlands Board of Tourism, PO Box 458, 2260 MG Leidschen-
dam. Tel: 070 370 5706.

Main Tourist Offices
Centraal Station, Amsterdam. Tel: 020 626 6444.
Den Hague CS, The Hague. Tel: 070 354 3501.

State Employment Service
Singel 202, 1016 AA Amsterdam. Tel: 020 520 0911.
Begynenhof 8, 5611 EL Eindhoven. Tel: 040 325325.
Engelse Kamp 4, 9722 AX Groningen. Tel: 050 225911.
Troelstrakade 65, 2531 AA The Hague.
Schiedamse Vest 160, 3011 BH Rotterdam.

Private Employment Agencies
Manpower, Van Baerlestraat 16, Amsterdam. Tel: 020 664 4180.
Vedior Hotel Service, Leidsestraat 24, Amsterdam. Tel: 020 271116.

Newspapers
De Telegraaf, De Volkskrant, Het Parool (Amsterdam), *Haagsche
Courant* (The Hague), *Utrechts Nieuwsblad* (Utrecht).

Language courses
Linguaphone, 124 Brompton Road, London SW3 2TL. Tel: 0800
282417.

Other contacts
Central Bureau Arbeidsvoorziening, PO Box 437, 2280 AR Rijswijk.
(Can find and advise on temporary work for young people; all
types of industry.)
EXIS, Centre for International Youth Activities, PO Box 152344,
1001 MH Amsterdam. (Can find and advise on temporary work for
young people; all types of industry.)
Rotterdam and Lower Maas Chamber of Commerce and Industry,
Postbus 30 025, 3001 DA Rotterdam. Tel: 041 45022. (Can advise
on acceptability of foreign qualifications, for certain areas of work.)
Uitgeverij Intermediair, Postbus 3434, 1001 Amsterdam. (Publishes a
weekly job bulletin, called Intermediair, and an annual yearbook of
opportunities. HND/graduate level.)

Some major hotels/groups
Golden Tulip Worldwide Hotels, Stationstraat 2, 1211 EM Hilversum.
Tel: 035 284588.

Work Experience Schemes
British Hospitality Association, 40 Duke Street, London W1M 6HR.
Tel: (0171) 499 6641.
Central Bureau for Educational Visits and Exchanges, Seymour
Mews House, Seymour Mews, London W1H 9PE. Tel: (0171) 486
5101.

Ireland

About hotel and catering in Ireland
The hospitality industry in Ireland is currently less developed than in
the UK. Although there are numerous international-class hotels in
Dublin, elsewhere the industry is still dominated by smaller family-
run concerns offering a high level of personal service. Operations
are, however, expanding fast. Several Irish companies, as well as
Forte from the UK, are developing modern chain restaurants and
hotel operations.

Types of work available
The fact that English is spoken in Ireland means that most of the jobs
discussed in Chapter 3 are available to people from the UK. Most UK
qualifications, including City & Guilds, are accepted by employers.

Sources to use
All the methods of finding a job, discussed in Chapter 4, may be
used.
Vacancies are advertised in UK as well as Irish newspapers. Both
the state employment agency, FAS, and private employment agencies
can be tried. Writing letters to prospective employers can also be
successful, although personal application is less successful due to the
very large area over which facilities are spread. An organisation
called CERT operates to further education, training and recruitment to
the Irish hospitality industry.

Visas and permits
UK citizens do not need a visa, work permit nor a residence permit to
live and work in Eire. However, you do need to take a full passport.

Other things you should know
Costs of living in Ireland are similar to or higher than the UK, although rates of pay are no higher. Income taxes are generally higher.
Unemployment is severe in some parts of the country, making much
competition for casual summer jobs.

Useful contacts
Embassies
Irish Embassy, 18 Grosvenor Place, London SW1X 7HR. Tel: (0171)
    235 2171.
British Embassy, 33 Merrion Road, Dublin 2. Tel: 01 764088.

Chambers of Commerce
The Chamber of Commerce of Ireland, 22 Merrion Square, Dublin 2.
    Tel: 01 612888.

Tourist Office in London
Ireland House, 150 Bond Street, London W1. Tel: (0171) 493 3201.

Tourist Authority
Irish Tourist Board, Baggot Street Bridge, Dublin 2. Tel: 01 676
    5871.

Main Tourist Offices
Grand Parade, Cork. Tel: 021 543289.
14 Upper O'Connell Street, Dublin. Tel: 01 747733.

State Employment Service
FAS, 65a Adelaide Road, Dublin 2. Tel: 01 765861.

Private Employment Agencies
A list is available from FAS.

Newspapers
The Irish Independent (see Thursday), *The Irish Times* (see Friday),
The Irish Press.

Other contacts
CERT, CERT House, Amiens Street, Dublin 1. Tel: 01 742555.
Community & Youth Information Centre, Sackville House, Sackville
    Place, Dublin 1. Tel: 01 786844. (Information on employment and
    exchanges for young people.)

Some major hotels/groups
Cie Tours International, 35 Lower Abbey Street, Dublin 1. Tel: 01
    703 1829.
Great Southern Hotels, 6 Charlemont Terrace, Dun Laoghaire. Tel: 01
    280 8031.

Jurys Hotel Group, Pembroke Road, Ballsbridge, Dublin 4. Tel: 01 605000.

Inter Hotels GB & Ireland, 35 Hogarth Road, London SW5 0QQ. Tel: (0171) 373 3241.

Killarney Hotels Ltd, Killarney, County Kerry. Tel: 064 31900.

Ryan Hotel Group, 23 Upper O'Connell Street, Dublin 1. Tel: 01 741114.

The Shelbourne, 27 St Stephens Green, Dublin 2. Tel: 01 766471.

The Old Ground Hotel, O'Connell Street, Ennis, County Clare. Tel: 065 28127.

Work Experience Schemes

British Hospitality Association, 40 Duke Street, London W1M 6HR. Tel: (0171) 499 6641.

Central Bureau for Educational Visits and Exchanges, Seymour Mews House, Seymour Mews, London W1H 9PE. Tel: (0171) 486 5101.

Turkey

About hotel and catering in Turkey

The hospitality industry in Turkey bears no similarity to the industry found in the UK, except for the substantial tourist industry which has developed in recent years. British visitors are the largest group, although Turkey is also popular with German and Scandinavian visitors.

The most visited parts of Turkey are along the south east coast, especially resorts such as Altinkum, Kusadasi, Bodrum, Gumbet, Marmaris and Olu Deniz. Istanbul is also a popular destination for city breaks. In general, however, hotel and catering facilities are still underdeveloped and far behind those in France and Spain.

Types of work available

Most of the UK tour operators do not employ hotel and catering staff. There are a small number of sailing holiday operators who require yacht crew, maintenance staff, couriers, hosts/hostesses and cooks. See *How to Get a Job in Travel and Tourism* for more details of this. Most opportunities are for summer casual work only.

Sources to use

The only effective method of pre-arranging a job is to write to employers direct. No employment agencies can help foreigners and newspapers are also of little use, although there is an English language newspaper in Istanbul.

Visas and permits
As Turkey is not a member of the European Union, all UK citizens wishing to work there must obtain a working visa. This is applied for by your employer once you have found a job. Those entering as tourists may look for work but may not actually work until a working visa is issued. Some people work illegally on a tourist visa. A tourist visa is required by all UK tourists visiting Turkey and is issued at the border or airport.

Other things you should know
Turkey has a very low cost of living. Wages are also much lower than the UK and employers are not always reliable about making payment. It is not necessary to speak any Turkish to find work. There is intense competition for most jobs and so it is better to only look for those jobs where being able to speak fluent English is required.

Useful contacts
Embassies
Turkish Embassy, 43 Belgrave Square, London SW1X 8PA. Tel: (0171) 235 5222.
British Embassy, Sehit Ersan Caddesi 46a, Ankara. Tel: 04 127 4310.

Chambers of Commerce
British Chamber of Commerce, PO Box 190 Karaköy, Istanbul.

Tourist Office in London
170-173 Piccadilly, London W1V 9DD. Tel: (0171) 734 8681.

Tourist Authority
Ministry of Tourism, Gazi Mustafa Kemal Bul. 87, Demirlepe, Ankara. Tel: 04 230 1861.

Main Tourist Offices
Divanyolu Caddesi, Istanbul. Tel: 01 522 4903.
Iskele Meydani, Bodrum.

Newspapers
Daily News (English language newspaper.)

Language courses
Berlitz, 79 Wells Street, London W1A 3BZ. Tel: (0171) 637 0330.
Inlingua, 8-10 Rotton Park Road, Birmingham B16 9JJ. Tel: (0121) 454 0204.

Work Experience Schemes
Enquire about possibilities with:
Central Bureau for Educational Visits and Exchanges, Seymour Mews
House, Seymour Mews, London W1H 9PE. Tel: (0171) 486 5101.

Scandinavia: Denmark, Finland, Norway, Sweden

About hotel and catering in Scandinavia
The hotel and catering industries in the Scandinavian countries are
well developed and standards are high. Large hotels and modern
catering establishments (such as fast food) — those most likely to
employ foreign staff — tend to be located in the cities and in the
more densely populated southernmost parts of Norway, Sweden and
Finland.

Opportunities in this region should increase substantially in future
as Finland, Norway and Sweden have joined the European Economic
Area (EEA). This will lead to eventual membership of the EU and
subsequent removal of work permit restrictions for those from the EU
countries.

Types of work available
It is difficult for foreigners to get permanent work in hotels and restaurants in the Scandinavian countries. Most of the opportunities are
in casual work in tourist-related facilities, especially in hotels, restaurants and bars.

Denmark has a number of summer beach resorts, and Copenhagen
is a very popular resort city. Oslo is a popular tourist city, whilst
Lillehammer in Norway is Scandinavia's only ski resort of any size.
Cruising on the Norwegian fjords attracts many tourists, and tours are
operated to Lapland, above the Arctic Circle.

Stockholm in Sweden and Helsinki in Finland receive only small
numbers of visitors. The southern coast of Sweden is a popular tourist
spot, as is the island of Gotland.

Sources to use
The main sources to use are the state employment agencies, newspapers, and direct application to employers, using the tourist offices
as a source of addresses for hotels etc. There are many private employment agencies in Denmark but few elsewhere.

Visas and permits
UK citizens do not need a work permit to work in Denmark, but
should obtain a residence permit from the Department for the Super-

vision of Aliens within three months of arrival. In other countries a work permit may be needed before leaving the UK, although this requirement is being phased out under the EEA agreement between the EU and the Scandinavian countries. Check the current situation with the relevant Embassy.

Other things you should know
All the Scandinavian countries are substantially more expensive to live in than the UK; accommodation is particularly expensive. Rates of income tax are high.

Denmark

Danish Embassy, 55 Sloane Square, London SW1X 9SR. Tel: (0171) 333 0200.
British Embassy, Kastelvej 38-40, 2100 Copenhagen. Tel: 33 246600.
Danish Tourist Office, Sceptre House, 169-173 Regent Street, London SW1X 9SR. Tel: (0171) 235 1255.
Denmark Tourist Board, Vesterbrogade 6D, 1620 Copenhagen V. Tel: 33 111415.

Main Tourist Offices
8 Osterå, Aalborg.
22 H.C. Andersen Boulevard, Copenhagen. Tel: 33 111325.
Skolegade 33, Esbjerg. Tel: 75 124258.

State employment agency
Arbejdsformidlingen, Adelgade 13, Copenhagen 1304.

Newspapers
Politiken, Ekstra Bladet, Den Bla Auis, Belingske Tidende, Det Fri Aktuelt, Fryens Stiftstidente, Vestkysten.

Other contacts
Use-It Youth Information Centre, Rådhusstraende 13, 1446 Copenhagen K. (Information on casual work for young people.)

Work Experience Schemes
British Hospitality Association, 40 Duke Street, London W1M 6HR. Tel: (0171) 499 6641.
Central Bureau for Educational Visits and Exchanges, Seymour Mews House, Seymour Mews, London W1H 9PE. Tel: (0171) 486 5101.

Finland

Finnish Embassy, 38 Chesham Place, London SW1X 8HW. Tel: (0171) 235 9531.

British Embassy, Itainen Puistotie 17, 00140 Helsinki. Tel: 90 661293.

Finnish Tourist Office, 66 Haymarket, London SW1Y 4RF. Tel: (0171) 839 4048.

Main Tourist Offices
Pohjoiseplanadi 19, Helsinki. Tel: 90 1693757.
Hatanpään, Tampere.
Käsityöläiskatu 3, Turku.

State employment agency
Ministry of Labour, Fabianinkatu 32, 00100 Helsinki 10.

Newspapers
Turun Sanomat, Aamulehti, Helsingin Sanomat.

Norway

Norwegian Embassy, 39 Eccleston Street, London SW1W 9NT. Tel: (0171) 730 9900.

British Embassy, Thomas Heftyesgate 8, 0244 Oslo 2. Tel: 02 55 24 99.

Norwegian Tourist Office, 5 Lower Regent Street, London W1. Tel: (0171) 839 6255.

Norwegian Tourist Board, PO Box 499, Sentrum, 0105 Oslo 1. Tel: 02 42 70 44.

Main Tourist Offices
Torgallmenning, Bergen. Tel: 05 31 32 75.
Rådhusplassen, Oslo. Tel: 02 83 00 50.
Torvet, Trondheim. Tel: 07 53 04 90.

State employment agency
Arbeidsdirektoratet, Holbergs Plass 7, Postboks 8127 Dep, Oslo 1. Tel: 01 11 10 70.

Newspapers
Dagbladet, Aftenposten, Arbeiderbladet.

Work Experience Schemes
Make enquiries with:
Atlantis Youth Exchange, Rolf Hofmosgate 18, 0655 Oslo 6.

Sweden

Swedish Embassy, 11 Montagu Place, London W1H 2AL. Tel: (0171)
    724 2101.
British Embassy, Skarpögatan, 11527 Stockholm. Tel: 08 667 0149.
Swedish Tourist Office, 3 Cork Street, London W1X 1HA. Tel:
    (0171) 437 5816.
Swedish Tourist Board, Kungsträdgarden, Box 7473, 10392 Stock-
    holm. Tel: 08 790 3100.

Main Tourist Offices
Kungsportsplatsen, Gothenburg.
Färjeleden 3, Visby, Gotland. Tel: 0489 16933.
Västra Boulevarden, Kristianstad.
Norrmalm, Stockholm. Tel: 08 789 2000.

State employment agency
Arbetmarknadsstryrelsen, Box 2021, 12612 Stockholm.

Newspapers
*Svenska Dagbladet, Dagen, Expressen, Dagnes Nyheter, Göteborg
Posten.*

Some major hotels/groups (all of Scandinavia)
Best Western Finland, Annankatu 29A, 00100 Helsinki, Finland. Tel:
    90 694 7755.
Grand Hotels, Vesterbrogade 9, 1620 Copenhagen, Denmark. Tel: 31
    31 36 00.
Reso Hotels, St. Eriksgaten 115, 11392 Stockholm, Sweden. Tel: 08
    728 3200.
Summer Hotels, Yrjökau 38, 00100 Helsinki, Finland. Tel: 90 693
    1347.

EASTERN EUROPE

Bulgaria, Czech Republic, Hungary, Poland, Romania, Russia.

About hotel and catering in Eastern Europe
The hospitality industry in eastern Europe is growing steadily. Not
only is there more demand for these services, but hotels and restaurants are very popular business projects for the many new entrepre-
neurs in this part of the world.

Having said this, it is important to realise that the potential for
finding work in eastern Europe is still quite small. There is an ample

pool of cheap, local labour. Few hotels and restaurants can afford to hire comparatively expensive help from the west.

At the moment most of the largest and most successful new hotels and restaurants are either owned by western companies, or are partnerships between western and eastern European companies. For example, Forte have recently relaunched the Hotel Bristol in Warsaw, Poland, and Forte Agip are developing interests in Hungary.

Types of work available
It is difficult for foreigners to take most of the jobs in these countries owing to work permit restrictions and language problems. So, for example, casual hotel and catering work is not usually possible. Most of the jobs available are more senior management and supervisory jobs with the larger hotels only, especially those operated by western companies or western partners.

Sources to use
Write to companies, including European partners. A small number of vacancies appear in the national newspapers, *Caterer and Hotel-keeper*, and *Overseas Jobs Express*. There are no suitable employment agencies and personal visits are unlikely to be successful.

Visas and permits
Work permits and visas are needed for all these countries. These will be arranged by employer once you have found a job.

Other things you should know
Rates of pay in eastern Europe are extremely low, although those working for western companies will receive western rates. In most places facilities are still way behind the rest of Europe.

Bulgaria

Bulgarian Embassy, 186 Queen's Gate, London SW7 5HL. Tel: (0171) 584 9400.
British Embassy, Boulevard Marshal Tolbukin 65-67, Sofia. Tel: 02 879575.
Bulgarian Tourist Office, 18 Prince's Street, London W1R 7HE. Tel: (0171) 499 6988.

Czech Republic

Czech Embassy, 25 Kensington Palace Gardens, London W8 4QY. Tel: (0171) 727 3966.

British Embassy, Mala Strana, Thunovska Ulice 14, 12550 Prague 1.
Tel: 02 533347.
Czech Tourist Office, 17-18 Old Bond Street, London W1X 8RB. Tel:
(0171) 629 6058.

Hungary

Hungarian Embassy, 35 Eaton Place, London SW1X 8BY. Tel: (0171)
235 2664.
British Embassy, Harmincad Utca 6, Budapest V. Tel: 1 118 2888.
Hungarian Tourist Office, 6 Conduit Street, London W1R 9TG. Tel:
(0171) 493 0263.

State Employment Service
Katona J. Utca 25, Budapest. Tel: 1 122 294.
Bokány D. Utca 2a, Budapest. Tel: 1 124 630.
Széchenyi Tér 9, Pécs. Tel: 72 13 721.
Bajcsy Zs. Utca 4, Szeged. Tel: 62 22 890.
Csaba Utca 26, Györ. Tel: 96 11 180.

Poland

Polish Embassy, 47 Portland Place, London W1N 3AG. Tel: (0171)
580 5481.
British Embassy, 1 Aleja Róz, 00556 Warsaw. Tel: 02 228 1001.
Polish Tourist Office, 82 Mortimer Street, London W1N 7DE. Tel:
(0171) 580 8028.

Romania

Romanian Embassy, 4 Palace Green, London W8 4QD. Tel: (0171)
937 9666.
British Embassy, 24 Strada Jules Michelet, 70154 Bucharest. Tel: 01
111634.
Romanian Tourist Office, 17 Nottingham Place, London W1M 3FF.
Tel: (0171) 224 3692.

Russia

Russian Embassy, 13 Kensington Palace Gardens, London W8 4QX.
Tel: (0171) 229 3628.
British Embassy, Naberezhnaya Morisa Toreza 14, Moscow. Tel: 095
231 8511.
Russian Tourist Office (Intourist), 219 Marsh Wall, London E14 9JF.
Tel: (0171) 538 8600.

Other contacts (all Eastern Europe)
Some major hotels/groups
AGIP Forte International, Via Valentino Mazola 66, 00142 Rome, Italy.
Almatur U1. Ordynacka 9, 00364 Warsaw, Poland. Tel: 022 26 84 04.
Cedok Travel and Hotel Corp, Na Prikope 18, 11135 Prague 1, Czech Republic. Tel: 02 2117 111.
Grand Hotel Europe, Nevski Prospekt, 191073 St Petersburg, Russia. (Mail to: PO Box 53, 53501 Lappeenranta, Finland.)
Hotel Bristol, U1. Krakowskie Przedmiéscie 42/44, 00325 Warsaw, Poland. Tel: 039 121061.
HungarHotels, Petofi Su 14, 1052 Budapest V, Hungary. Tel: 0361 1182 033.
Las Vegas Casino Hotels, 131 Marija Luiza Boulevard, Sofia, Bulgaria. Tel: 397422.
Orbis, U1. Bracka 16, 00028 Warsaw, Poland. Tel: 022 26 02 71.
Pamporovo Resort, 4870 Pamporovo, Bulgaria. Tel: 03021 236.
Riviera Holiday Club, Golden Sands, Bulgaria. Tel: 52 85 52 15.
Sports-Tourist, U1. Grochowska 280, 00987 Warsaw, Poland. Tel: 022 13 23 86.
Sunny Beach Resort, 8240 Slanchev Briag, Bulgaria. Tel: 0554 2305.

Work Experience Schemes
Make enquiries with:
Central Bureau for Educational Visits and Exchanges, Seymour Mews House, Seymour Mews, London W1H 9PE. Tel: (0171) 486 5101.
Commission of the European Communities, 8 Storey's Gate, London SW1P 3AT. Tel: (0171) 973 1992.

USA AND CANADA

About hotel and catering in these countries
The countries of north America all have very large and very well-developed hotel and catering industries, with seemingly good potential for employment. However, the main problem is that all countries in this region impose strict visa requirements and this makes it extremely difficult for foreigners to work in, for example, Miami, or on a Caribbean island.

Unless you can find an employer willing to employ you, with no one else locally able to do that work (which is very unlikely), then your chances of obtaining a visa are extremely remote. There are, however, three restricted areas of work in which it may be possible to find a job and which are covered here.

Types of work available
- *Cruise lines.* Miami is the world's biggest cruise ship port with dozens of arrivals and departures each week. As crew work on short contracts there is a continuous requirement for new staff. Because these jobs are at sea, and not actually in any particular country, there are no visa restrictions.

- *Summer camps for children.* Working in a summer camp, in either the USA or Canada, entitles suitable participants to a special work visa. Jobs are available in several catering occupations.

- *Exchange and work experience opportunities.* The Association of International Practical Training (AIPT) can arrange a period of work in the USA for suitable applicants. The age limit is 19-35 and you must have experience in the hospitality industry in the UK and/or a hotel and catering qualification, or be studying for one.

Details are available from: Central Bureau for Educational Visits and Exchanges, Seymour Mews House, Seymour Mews, London W1H 9PE. Tel: (0171) 486 5101.

More information about jobs with cruise lines, and in summer camps, is given in *How to Get a Job in Travel and Tourism.*

Sources to use
For jobs in these countries it is advisable to apply direct to employers from the UK first. Some vacancies are advertised in the national newspapers and *Overseas Jobs Express.*

Visas and permits
You must have a working visa to take up a job in the USA or Canada (cruise jobs excepted). This can only be applied for, to the appropriate Embassy, once you have found a job and before travelling to the country concerned.

Other things you should know
Although a wide range of other work in hotels and catering is available in these countries, it is illegal to undertake it without a working visa. This is very difficult to obtain.

Canada

Canadian High Commission, Trafalgar Square, London SW1Y 5BJ. Tel: (0171) 629 9492.

British High Commission, Elgin Street, Ottawa K1P 5K7. Tel: 0613 237 1530.

Canadian Tourist Programme, Trafalgar Square, London SW1Y 5BJ. Tel: (0171) 629 9492.

Tourism Industry Association of Canada, 130 Albert Street, Suite 1016, Ottawa ONKP 5G4. Tel: 0613 238 3883.

Provincial information offices
Alberta: 1 Mount Street, London W1Y 5AA.
British Columbia: 1 Regent Street, London SW1Y 4NS.
Nova Scotia: 14 Pall Mall, London SW1Y 5LU.
Quebec: 59 Pall Mall, London SW1Y 5HJ.
Ontario: 21 Knightsbridge, London SW1Y 7LY.
Saskatchewan: 16 Berkeley Street, London W1X 5AE.

Other contacts
Some major hotels/groups
Canadian Pacific Hotels, 1 University Avenue, Suite 1400, Toronto M5S 2K9. Tel: 416 367 7111.
Four Seasons Hotels and Resorts, 1165 Leslie Street, Don Mills, Ontario M3C 2K8. Tel: 416 449 1750.

USA

United States Embassy, 24 Grosvenor Square, London W1V 2JB. Tel: (0171) 499 9000.

Visa Branch, 5 Upper Grosvenor Street, London W1A 2JB. Tel: (0171) 499 3443.

British Embassy, 3100 Massachusetts Avenue NW, Washington DC 20009. Tel: 202 462 1340.

US Travel and Tourism Administration, Washington DC 20230. Tel: 202 377 0136.

Tourist office contacts in USA
Alaska: Tel: 907 465 2020.
California: Tel: 916 322 1396.
Florida: Tel: 904 487 1462.
Hawaii: Tel: 808 923 1811.
Massachusetts: Tel: 617 727 3201.
Mississippi: Tel: 1 800 647 2290.
New York: Tel: 518 474 4116.
Texas: Tel: 512 475 5956.
Washington DC: Tel: 202 789 7000.

Other contacts
Some major hotels/groups
Fairmont Hotels, Atop Nob Hill, 950 Mason Street, San Francisco CA94016. Tel: 415 772 5000.
Forte Hotels Inc, 1973 Friendship Drive, El Cajon CA92020. Tel: 619 448 1884.
Guest Quarters Suite, 30 Rowes Wharf, Boston MA02110. Tel: 617 330 1440.
Holiday Inns, 3 Ravinia Drive, Suite 2000, Atlanta GA30346. Tel: 040 604 2000.
Howard Johnson Franchises, 339 Jefferson Road, Parsipanny NJ07054. Tel: 201 428 9700.
Hyatt Hotels, Madison Plaza, 200 West Madison Street, Chicago IL60606. Tel: 312 750 1234.
Leading Hotels of the World, 747 Third Avenue, New York NY10017-2847. Tel: 212 838 7874.
Marriot Hotels, 1 Marriot Drive, Washington DC20058. Tel: 301 380 9000.
Preferred Hotels, 1901 South Meyers Road, Suite 220, Oakbrook Terrace IL60181. Tel: 708 953 0404.
Radisson Hotels International, Carlson Parkway, PO Box 59159, Minneapolis MN55459-8204. Tel: 612 540 5526.
Ramada International Hotels, 2655 Le Jeene Road, Coral Gables FL33134. Tel: 305 460 1900.
Sheraton Hotels, Inns and Resorts, 60 State Street, Boston MA02109. Tel: 617 367 3600.
Westin Hotels and Resorts, 2001 Sixth Avenue, Seattle WA98121. Tel: 206 443 5000.

AUSTRALIA AND NEW ZEALAND

About hotel and catering in these countries
Australia and New Zealand have well developed hospitality industries, but there is a great contrast between the populated areas and elsewhere. The city and resort areas of Australia have many international class hotels and restaurants, whereas remote areas only have very basic facilities.

It is extremely difficult to get a visa to live and work in both Australia and New Zealand. However, exceptions are made for young people aged 18-25 who can get a 12 month working holiday visa allowing them to take a temporary job in Australia.

Types of work available
Those who have experience of hotel and catering work should be able

to get any job in hospitality in Australia. Those without experience can try for casual work in hotels, bars and restaurants, but the competition for these jobs is considerable.

The main areas for tourism in Australia are Sydney and the coastal resorts in the north eastern state of Queensland, such as Gold Coast and Surfer's Paradise. In New Zealand, Auckland and the North Island are most popular with tourists.

Sources to use
It is difficult to arrange jobs in advance and this is best done on arrival. Use newspapers and also direct approaches to employers. It is also a good idea to use private employment agencies and, in Australia, the state employment agency called CES.

Visas and permits
It is extremely difficult to secure permanent residence in Australia. Visas are awarded according to a points system which takes account of your age, status, skills and qualifications. A one year working holiday visa is much easier to obtain. You must be aged 18-30, with at least £2,000 capital, and intending to stay in Australia for no more than one year and then return. The cost of this is A$130. Details are available from the Australian High Commission. It is not possible to get work visas once in Australia.

The New Zealand authorities will consider applications for work permits from people who find a job in New Zealand. However, the number of permits issued has reduced considerably in recent years.

Other things you should know
Australia and New Zealand have similar costs and standards of living to the UK; wages are about the same or higher. Unemployment is a problem in both countries.

Australia

Australian High Commission, Australia House, Strand, London WC2B 4LA. Tel: (0171) 379 4334.
British High Commission, Commonwealth Avenue, Canberra ACT 2600. Tel: 06 270 6666.
Australian Tourist Commission, Gemini House, 10-18 Putney Hill, London SW15 6AA. Tel: (0181) 780 1424.

Australian Agents-General in London
New South Wales: 75 King William Street, London EC4N 7HA.
Queensland: 392 Strand, London WC2R 0LZ.
South Australia: 50 Strand, London WC2N 5LW.
Victoria: Victoria House, Melbourne Place, Strand, London WC2B
    4LG.
Western Australia: 115 Strand, London WC2R 0AJ.

State Employment Services (CES)
45 Grenfell Street, Adelaide.
215 Adelaide Street, Brisbane.
128 Bourke Street, Melbourne.
818-820 George Street, Sydney.
186 St George's Terrace, Perth.

Private Employment Agencies
ECCO, 18 Bent Street, Sydney.
Drake Personnel, 9 Queen Street, Melbourne.

Newspapers
Sydney Morning Herald (Sydney), *Courier & Mail* (Brisbane), *The
West Australian* (Adelaide), *The Melbourne Age* (Melbourne).

Other contacts
Some major hotels/groups
Federal Pacific Hotels and Casinos, 167 Collins Street, Melbourne
    VIC3000. Tel: 03 654 4133.
Southern Pacific Hotel Group Inc, PO Box 537, 709 New York Street,
    Sydney NSW2000. Tel: 02 290 3033.

New Zealand

New Zealand High Commission, New Zealand House, Haymarket,
    London SW1Y 4TQ. Tel: (0171) 973 0366.
British High Commission, 44 Hill Street, PO Box 1812, Wellington 1.
    Tel: 09 472 6049.
New Zealand Tourist Board, New Zealand House, Haymarket,
    London SW1Y 4TQ. Tel: (0171) 973 0360.

REST OF THE WORLD

Bahrain
Bahrain Embassy, 98 Gloucester Road, London SW7 4AU. Tel:
    (0171) 370 5132.

British Embassy, 21 Government Avenue, PO Box 114, Manama 306. Tel: 534404.

Brazil

Brazilian Embassy, 32 Green Street, London W1Y 4AT. Tel: (0171) 499 0877.

British Embassy, Setor de Embaixadus Sul, Quadra 801, Conjunto K, 70.408 Brazilia DF. Tel: 061 225 2710.

Brazilian Tourist Office, 35 Dover Street, London W1. Tel: (0171) 499 0877.

British and Commonwealth Chamber of Commerce, Caixa Postal 669ZC00, Sao Paulo.

Cyprus

Cyprus High Commission, 93 Park Street, London W1Y 4ET. Tel: (0171) 499 2810.

British High Commission, Alexander Pallis Street, PO Box 1978, Nicosia. Tel: 02 473131.

Cyprus Tourist Office, 213 Regent Street, London W1R 8DA. Tel: (0171) 734 9822.

Egypt

Egyptian Embassy, 26 South Street, London W1Y 6EL. Tel: (0171) 499 2401.

British Embassy, Ahmed Ragheb Street, Garden City, Cairo. Tel: 02 354 0850.

Egyptian Tourist Office, 168 Piccadilly, London W1Y 9DE. Tel: (0171) 493 5282.

Hong Kong

Hong Kong Government Office, 6 Grafton Street, London W1X 3LB. Tel: (0171) 499 3380.

Hong Kong Tourist Office, 125 Pall Mall, London SW1Y 5EA. Tel: (0171) 930 4775.

India

Indian Embassy, India House, Aldwych, London WC2B 4NA. Tel: (0171) 836 8484.

British High Commission, Chanakyapuri, New Delhi 21, 1100-21. Tel: 011 601371.

Indian Tourist Office, 7 Cork Street, London W1X 2AB. Tel: (0171) 629 0862.

Israel

Israeli Embassy, 2 Palace Green, London W8 4QB. Tel: (0171) 937 8050.

British Embassy, 192 Hayarkon Street, Tel Aviv. Tel: 03 524 9171.

Israel Tourist Office, 18 Great Marlborough Street, London W1V 1AF. Tel: (0171) 434 3651.

Japan

Japanese Embassy, 101-104 Piccadilly, London W1V 9FN. Tel: (0171) 465 6500.

British Embassy, 16 Kowa Building, 1-9-20 Akasaka, Minato-ku, Tokyo 107.

Japanese National Tourist Organisation, 167 Regent Street, London W1R 7FD. Tel: (0171) 734 9638.

Kenya

Kenyan High Commission, 45 Portland Place, London W1N 4AS. Tel: (0171) 636 2371.

British High Commission, PO Box 30133, Bruce House, Standard Street, Nairobi. Tel: 02 335944.

Kenyan Tourist Office, 13 New Burlington Street, London W1X 1FF. Tel: (0171) 839 4477.

Luxembourg

Luxembourg Embassy, 27 Wilton Crescent, London SW1X 8SD. Tel: (0171) 235 6961.

British Embassy, 14 Boulevard F.D. Roosevelt, 2450 Luxembourg. Tel: 29864

Malaysia

Malaysian High Commission, 45 Belgrave Square, London SW1X 8QT. Tel: (0171) 235 8033.

British High Commission, 185 Jalan Ampang, 50732 Kuala Lumpur. Tel: 03 248 2111.

Malaysian Tourist Office, 57 Trafalgar Square, London WC2N 5DU. Tel: (0171) 930 7932.

Mexico

Mexican Embassy, 8 Halkin Street, London SW1X 7DW. Tel: (0171) 235 6393.

British Embassy, Calle Rio Lerma 71, Colonia Cuauhtémoc, 06500 Mexico City, DF. Tel: 05 207 20 89.

Mexican Tourist Office, 7 Cork Street, London W1X 1PB. Tel: (0171) 434 1058.

British Chamber of Commerce, Tiber 103, Cuauhtémoc, Mexico City 06500 DF.

Morocco

Moroccan Embassy, 49 Queen's Gate, London SW7 5NE. Tel: (0171) 581 5001.

British Embassy, 17 Boulevard de la Tour Hassan, BP45, Rabat. Tel: 720905.

Moroccan Tourist Office, 174 Regent Street, London W1R 6HB. Tel: (0171) 437 0073.

Singapore

Singapore High Commission, 9 Wilton Crescent, London SW1X 8SA. Tel: (0171) 235 8315.

British High Commission, Tanglin Road, Singapore 1024. Tel: 473 9333.

Singapore Tourist Office, 33 Heddon Street, London W1R 7LB. Tel: (0171) 437 0033.

South Africa

South African Embassy, Trafalgar Square, London WC2N 5DP. Tel: (0171) 839 2211.

British Embassy, 6 Hill Street, Arcadia, Pretoria 0002. Tel: 012 433121.

South African Tourist Office, 1-4 Warwick Street, London W1R 5WB. Tel: (0171) 439 9661.

Thailand

Thai Embassy, 30 Queen's Gate, London SW7 5JB. Tel: (0171) 589 0173.

British Embassy, Wireless Road, Bangkok 10330. Tel: 02 235 0191.

Thailand Tourist Office, 9 Stafford Street, London W1X 3FE. Tel: (0171) 499 7679.

Tunisia

Tunisian Embassy, 29 Prince's Gate, London SW7 1QC. Tel: (0171) 584 8117.

British Embassy, BP229, 5 place de la Victoire, Tunis 1015RP. Tel: 01 245100.

Tunisian Tourist Office, 7a Stafford Street, London W1. Tel: (0171) 499 7679.

United Arab Emirates

UAE Embassy, 30 Prince's Gate, London SW7 1PT. Tel: (0171) 581 1281.

British Embassy, PO Box 248, Abu Dhabi. Tel: 326600.

Venezuela

Venezuelan Embassy, 1 Cromwell Road, London SW7 2HW. Tel: (0171) 584 4206.

British Embassy, Apartado 1246, Caracas 1010A. Tel: 02 751 1022.

Venezuelan Tourist Office, 1 Cromwell Road, London SW7 2HW. Tel: (0171) 584 4206.

Zambia

Zambian High Commission, 2 Palace Gate, London W8 5NG. Tel: (0171) 589 6655.

British High Commission, PO Box 50050, Independence Avenue, Lusaka. Tel: 01 228955.

Zambian Tourist Office, 163 Piccadilly, London W1V 9DE. Tel: (0171) 498 1188.

Zimbabwe

Zimbabwe High Commission, 429 Strand, London WC2R 0SA. Tel: (0171) 836 7755.

British High Commission, PO Box 4490, Stanley House, Jason Moyo Avenue (PO Box 4490), Harare. Tel: 04 793781.

Zimbabwe Tourist Office, 52-53 Piccadilly, London W1V 9AA. Tel: (0171) 629 3955.

Some major hotels/groups:

Amari Hotels & Resorts, 15th Floor, 500 Ploenchit Road, Bangkok, 10330 Thailand. Tel: 02 252 6118.

Dan Hotel Corp, 10 Kaufman Street, Tel Aviv 68012, Israel. Tel: 03 517 0033.

Goodwood Hotels Corp, Goodwood Park Hotel, 22 Scots Road, 0922 Singapore. Tel: 734 7176.

The Ashok Group, Jeevan Vihar, 3 Sansad Marg, New Delhi 110001, India. Tel: 011 310923.

Mandarin Oriental Hotel Group, 281 Gloucester Road, Causeway Bay, Hong Kong. Tel: 895 9288.

New Otani Hotels, 4-1 Kioi-cho, Choyoda-ku, Tokyo 102, Japan. Tel: 03 265 1111.

Nigeria Hotels Ltd, PO Box 895, 18 Club Road, Ikoyi, Lagos, Nigeria. Tel: 01 603200.

Nikko International Hotels, Jowa Yaesu Building, 4-1 Yaesu 2-chome, Chuo-ku, Tokyo 104, Japan. Tel: 033 3281 4321.

Oberoi Hotels, 7 Sham Nath Marg, Delhi 11054, India. Tel: 01 252 5464.

Othon Hotels, Rua Teolifo Otoni 15, Room 212, 20090 Rio de Janeiro, Brazil, Tel: 021 291 6111.

Peninsula Group, St. George's Building, Ice House Street, Hong Kong. Tel: 840 7788.

Regent International Hotels, 1513 New World Centre, Kowloon, Hong Kong. Tel: 366 3361.

Southern Sun Hotels, PO Box 5087, Johannesburg 2000, South Africa. Tel: 011 783 5330.

Taj Group of Hotels, Taj Mahal Hotel, Apollo Bunder, Bombay 400039, India. Tel: 022 202 3366.

Index

How to Pass That Interview
Judith Johnstone

Everyone knows how to succeed at interview: it's simple. Or is it? What makes the difference between success and failure? Is it just a matter of having the right qualifications or experience, turning up looking immaculately groomed and shaking hands in a positive manner? Not quite. When every candidate becomes a perfect clone of the one before, recruiters are looking for the candidate with 'something' extra to offer. This book shows how by thorough pre-interview preparation you can raise your chances of beating the competition, whether you are going for your first job interview, seeking a coveted place at the college of your choice, or wanting to present a good case to a business adviser on the road to self-employment.

128pp illus. 1 85703 118 0. Second edition.

How to Get That Job
Joan Fletcher

Now in a revised edition this popular book provides a clear step-by-step guide to identifying job opportunities, writing successful application letters, preparing for interviews, and being selected. 'A valuable book.' *Teachers Weekly.* 'Cheerful and appropriate . . . particularly helpful in providing checklists designed to bring system to searching for a job. This relaxed, friendly and very helpful little book could bring lasting benefit.' *Times Educational Supplement.* 'Clear and concise . . . should be mandatory reading by all trainees.' *Comlon Magazine (LCCI).* Joan Fletcher is an experienced Personnel Manager and Student Counsellor.

112pp illus. 1 85703 096 6. Third edition.

How to Master Business English
Michael Bennie

'An excellent book — not in the least dull . . . Altogether most useful for anyone seeking to improve their communication skills.' *IPS Journal.* 'Gives guidance on writing styles for every situation . . . steers the reader through the principles and techniques of effective letter-writing and document-planning.' *First Voice.* 'Useful chapters on grammar, punctuation and spelling. Frequent questionnaires and checklists enable the reader to check progress.' *Focus (Society of Business Teachers).*

208pp illus. 1 85703 129 6. Second edition.

How to Know Your Rights at Work
Robert Spicer

'Justifiably described as a practical guide to employment law. It is clearly written in language readily understood by the layman . . . The text has been well laid out and sections are clearly signposted . . . The extensive use of case study material is interesting and helpful . . . The book is not only relevant to

Careers Officers and their clients, but also to other people working in the employment/employment advisory field, eg Citizens Advice Bureaux workers, Personnel officers, Trade Union Personnel, and indeed anyone wishing to find out about their rights at work . . . The sort of book that can be easily dipped into for specific information, but which is interesting enough in its own right to be read from cover to cover.' *Careers Officer journal.* Robert Spicer MA(Cantab) is a practising barrister, legal editor and author who specialises in employment law.

141pp illus. 1 85703 009 5.

How to Get Into Films and TV
Robert Angell
Foreword by David Puttnam

Would you like to make a career in films or television? Whether you want to direct feature films, photograph documentaries, edit commercials or pop videos, write current affairs programmes for television, do art work for animation or just know that you want to be involved in film or television in some capacity but are not quite sure how to set about getting started, **How to Get Into Films and TV** will give you a wealth of information to guide you through the dense but exotic jungle with clear signposts to help you get a foot on the first rung of the ladder of these exciting industries. Robert Angell is a Council Member of the British Academy of Film & Television Arts (BAFTA) and Chairman of its Programme Committee and Short Film Award jury. The author of a British Film Institute Guide, *Film & TV: The Way In,* he also lectures on film and media studies at two London colleges.

144pp illus. 1 85703 105 9. Second edition.

How to Get a Job Abroad
Roger Jones BA(Hons) DipEd DPA

This popular title is essential reading for everyone planning to spend a period abroad. A key feature is the lengthy reference section of medium and long-term job opportunities and possibilities, arranged by region and country of the world, and by profession/occupation. There are more than 130 pages of specific contracts and leads, giving literally hundreds of addresses and much hard-to-find information. There is a classified guide to overseas recruitment agencies, and even a multi-lingual guide to writing application letters. 'A fine book for anyone considering even a temporary overseas job.' *The Evening Star.* 'A highly informative and well researched book . . . containing lots of hard information and a first class reference section . . . A superb buy.' *The Escape Committee Newsletter.* Roger Jones BA AKC DipTESL DipEd MInstAM DPA MBIM has himself worked abroad for many years and is a specialist writer on expatriate and employment matters.

272pp illus. 1 85703 115 6. Third edition.

How to Study Abroad
Teresa Tinsley BA DipEd

Studying abroad can open up a whole new horizon of opportunities, but what courses are available? How does one qualify? What does it cost? Can anyone do it? This book brings together a wealth of fascinating advice and reference information for everyone who has dreamed of pursuing a course of studies abroad, from art and archaeology to languages, music, science and technology.

176pp illus. 1 85703 083 4. Second edition.

How to Teach Abroad
Roger Jones BA(Hons) DipEd DPA

'An excellent book . . . An exhaustive and practical coverage of the possibilities and practicalities of teaching overseas.' *The Escape Committee Newsletter.*

192pp illus. 1 85703 108 3. Second edition.

How to Work from Home
Ian Phillipson

The Henley Centre for Forecasting estimates that 13% of the employed already spend at least some of their time working from home; other estimates suggest that with existing technology, as many as 7 million fulltime employees, 1.6 million part-timers and 1.3 million of the self-employed could all successfully work from home. Working from home is no longer a cottage industry. Improved technology, computers and faxes now allow professional, creative and business people of every kind to switch away from the traditional workplace and still communicate effectively with colleagues, suppliers and customers. This latest title in the HOW TO series provides a complete step-by-step guide to successful planning and organisation of what is increasingly becoming the preferred option for millions of individuals in the new work environment of the 1990s.

176pp illus. 1 85703 076 1.

How to Start a Business from Home
Graham Jones

Most people have dreamed of starting their own business from home at some time or other; but how do you begin? What special skills do you need? This great value-for-money paperback has the answers, showing how you can profit from your own talents and experience, and start turning spare time into cash from the comfort of your own home. It contains a wealth of ideas, projects, tips, facts, checklists and quick-reference information for everyone—whether in between jobs, taking early retirement, or students and others with time to invest. Packed with information on everything from choosing a good business idea and starting up to advertising, book-keeping and dealing with ofessionals, this book is essential reading for every budding entrepreneur. 'Full of ideas and advice.' *The Daily Mirror*. 'Full of excellent practical advice . . . Essential reading for anyone about to start their own home-based business.' *Own Base*. 'Packed with details and helpful advice.' *In Business Now (DTI)*. Graham Jones BSc(Hons) is an editor, journalist and lecturer specialising in practical business subjects.

176pp illus. 1 85703 126 1. Third edition.

How to Get a Job in America
Roger Jones BA(Hons) DipEd DPA

The United States has long been regarded as a land of opportunity, and millions of people around the world dream of landing a job there, despite the strict immigration controls now in force. This book helps you to turn your dream into reality by explaining the work possibilities open to non-US citizens. Drawing on the experiences of individuals, companies and recruitment agencies Roger Jones reveals the range of jobs available, the locations, pay and conditions, and how to get hired. The book includes the latest on immigration procedures following the 1990 US Immigration Act. This is an essential handbook for everyone planning to work in the US, whether on a short-term vacation assignment, on secondment or contract, or on a permanent basis. Roger Jones is a freelance author specialising in careers and expatriate matters and has himself worked overseas.

224pp illus. 1 85703 110 5. Second edition.

How to Get a Job in Australia
Nick Vandome

With ever-increasing competition for entry into Australia and its employment market it is essential for migrant job-hunters to arm themselves with as much practical and relevant information as possible. This handbook provides a complete step-by-step guide to all aspects of job-finding in Australia, for both casual and permanent employment. Where to look for work, what pay and conditions to expect, and the current economic climate is explained alongside key information about tax, contracts, your rights at work and the Australian philosophy of employment; all you need to know to earn your Aussie dollars. Nick Vandome is a freelance writer who has himself worked and travelled extensively in Australia. He has written articles for several Australian publications including *The Melbourne Age,* and is author of **How to Spend a Year Abroad** in this series.

176pp illus. 1 85703 048 6.